WELL MADE DECISIONS

MAY ALL YOUR
DECISIONS BE
WELL MADE!

D1572123

WELL MADE DECISIONS

JENNIFER DAVIS

NEW DEGREE PRESS

WELL MADE DECISIONS

ISBN   978-1-63676-747-5   *Paperback*

          978-1-63730-491-4   *Kindle Ebook*

          978-1-63730-492-1   *Ebook*

CONTENTS

———

INTRODUCTION

———

Why couldn't it just be easy?

The call came on Tuesday afternoon from the founder of Clarity Visual Systems, Paul Gulick. The next day, Planar Systems would acquire his company, and we were finalizing the presentation he would give to his employees after the public announcement.

Momentum had been building for this deal for some time. Lawyers, bankers, and a host of functional subject-matter experts had participated in a due diligence process to bring us to this point. They had produced and reviewed reams of documents. Scenarios were modeled and vetted, and assumptions documented. A lot of work had gone into making a decision defined by the acquisition agreement that executives would soon sign.

Planar was a publicly traded company that spent years manufacturing embedded display components for medical devices, industrial equipment, and fuel dispensers. We were rapidly expanding into other high-growth market categories. This had led us down a nonorganic growth path, including this acquisition, which I helped lead in my strategy role.

I worked on the messages we would deliver to employees, customers, suppliers, the industry, and the local media once the ink was dry on that contract. I was briefed by our legal counsel and chief financial officer about what could and couldn't be said. All presentations and documents would be disclosed to investors, per Security and Exchange Commission (SEC) guidelines, and sensitivities abounded.

As my phone rang, I recognized the number. The knot in my stomach told me this was going to be a tough conversation.

As I went through the proposed employee presentation with Clarity's founder, I had a lot of edits. It was an embarrassing number of edits.

Forward-looking statement had to be removed. Enthusiastic adjectives had to be tempered. His frustration level rose as my red ink flowed.

With a quick smile and sharp wit, Gulick was a leader that people enjoyed following. "Yes" was a word he was accustomed to hearing. That day, I was the person, it seems, who could only say "no."

"You are turning this into a content-free presentation," I recall him musing. He wasn't wrong. What added to the irritation was we were under a deadline. It was getting very real, very fast. In a few short hours, he was signing away ownership of his company. Now many things were no longer his decision. He would be an employee, not an owner; an employee of a publicly traded company, no less. He was not even allowed to decide what to say to his own employees about what might have been one of the biggest decisions of his career.

Planar had decided to acquire Clarity with the information we had. As you will hear more throughout this book, there is no doubt the capabilities, talent, and channel access Clarity brought to Planar was critical to the company's future success. But on that afternoon, all we had was our best attempt and our good intentions. Would it be enough?

Do you know what percentage of acquisitions are well-intentioned? One hundred percent. No one goes through that much work for no reason or a futile outcome (at least, I would hope not). Yet, 70-90 percent of acquisitions *fail* to achieve their intended potential. Thinking back on that Tuesday night, I had no way of truly knowing if the purchase of Clarity would be the right decision: whether we would become a statistic or buck the trend. But one thing was sure. We were determined to *make* it right, starting with this presentation to employees.

From my vantage point, with tasks on both sides of that announcement, I could see so clearly the acquisition decision wasn't just the finish line of this extensive due diligence process or another milestone in a serial entrepreneur's journey. The acquisition was the starting line of something new. It was the beginning of new workstreams, new leadership, new possibilities, new constraints, and new choices that would come in rapid succession over the coming hours, days, weeks, and years that would prove out the value of the decision. I was shepherding in the new, and it felt hard because it was.

Later most would agree the acquisition was a good decision. The CEO and others in leadership were praised for making such an astute move. It was the *right* decision. But I knew the truth. It *became* the right decision because of what started happening on Wednesday once employees, customers, and suppliers were told and started working together toward the new future.

I made a commitment to myself in that acquisition to stay aware throughout the hectic implementation to see what I could learn. Since then, I have done the same through dozens of major strategy pivots or product introductions. In each case, a familiar pattern has emerged: a flurry of activity proceeds a convergent act of decision making where data and emotion run hand in hand. After the point of convergence comes divergence: the expanding and extending flow of follow-on action, implementation, activation, conversation, negotiation, and, yes, more decisions. That is the messy part we are quick to forget or overlook.

This book exists because I realized something was missing from the business journals and books on my shelf, the degrees on my wall, and from my own writing over the years. Something was hidden in plain sight and made all the difference for organizations and their leaders.

> How we perceive decisions in hindsight is not really about the decision, but what happened after the decision was made.

You might be wondering why I chose to write about decisions and then start it off by saying they don't matter? It isn't that decisions don't matter. It is that they matter differently than you might think. That difference defines the success you will achieve through your decisions.

There is a common myth of an inventor who is sitting alone when inspiration strikes. The idea is that innovation is born in a burst of energy and clarity. Thomas Edison, who himself was equal parts showman and inventor, reportedly said genius was "1 percent inspiration and 99 percent perspiration." I believe the same can be said about decisions.

Decisions are 1 percent inspiration and 99 percent perspiration, and the overwhelming majority of sweat-inducing work happens *after* the decision, not before. This doesn't diminish the thought and effort that goes into the choices we make as a leader. It just reflects the broader reality of the work that makes our decisions successful and, in turn, makes our businesses successful. If we focus only on the 1 percent, as tempting as it may be, we can virtually guarantee bad outcomes.

For people who make their living making decisions—and most of us do in one capacity or another—the myth of a solitary good (or bad) decision is not only inaccurate. It is dangerous. It focuses us on the 1 percent and glosses over the 99 percent.

I have worked for six CEOs or presidents in my career, have held C-suite roles at publicly traded global companies, and served on boards and committees. The preparation of this book afforded me the gift of additional self-reflection and the ability to vet my assumptions with other leaders across industries. In business, we are all in a race with no finish line, and I am pleased to share with you some of what I have learned in pursuit.

What I have seen in my career is genius in business decision making is only partially about making choices. It is much more about courage, humility, curiosity, creativity, culture, and even strategic compromise. We can oversimplify and perpetuate the myths that keep companies and their leaders from achieving their potential. Or we can take the real-life stories and pro tips in this book and turn our businesses into a maker studio where we use all our tools, resources, and creativity to make decisions right.

On a different Tuesday afternoon, I took a break from my writing and browsed a home interiors magazine. There I found an interview with Kevin Sharkey, the senior vice president and executive editorial director with Martha Stewart Living Omnimedia. The interviewer asked him, "Are there elements of your home's interior design that extend to your personal style?" He replied, "Well, similar to my home, my style, I think, is appropriate. It's well made. And it's considered." Those words jumped off the page to me.

Appropriate

Considered

Well made

Isn't that what we are all striving for in our decisions? This captured well my motivation to write and what I thought was at stake for all of us.

So, for all the business leaders who pick up this book on a Tuesday afternoon, I hope it can prepare you for a future of well-made decisions.

CHAPTER 1:

MAKING HARD DECISIONS EASY

———

"Those are the things an entrepreneur needs—an open mind and the ability to see the world with new eyes."

—CATERINA FAKE, COFOUNDER OF FLICKR AND HUNCH

A new CEO comes into her office and finds three envelopes left by the previous leader with a note: "When you encounter trouble on the job, open an envelope and follow the instructions."

She had forgotten about the envelopes stashed in the drawer until a few quarters later, when the business returned horrible results and earnings did not meet analyst estimates. She opened the envelope labeled "one," and inside was a note: "Blame the previous CEO." She thought that was a pretty good idea and made sure to mention the previous leader's poor inventory controls and risky innovation investments in the investor call. The stock rebounded. Crisis was averted.

About a year later, the business hit another rough patch, and she opened the second envelope. The instructions read: "Reorganize." She promptly moved from a business unit structure to a functional one, took out some costs, and made it easier for customers to buy multiple product categories.

Things were going well until a few years later when the business faced an economic downturn. The CEO opened the third envelope and read the card. It said: "Make three new envelopes."

We often think of decisions in this same way – an envelope to be opened, a task to be completed, or a catalyst that requires a response. After all, when faced with a decision, we seek to reach a *conclusion*. This implies a decision is the end of something.

Or is it? It is easy to believe so. A doctor analyzes a patient's symptoms or test results and comes back with a decision called a *diagnosis*. This marks the end of what might have been months or years of wondering, pain, or inconclusive testing. A diagnosis has a finality to it. Similarly, a jury considers evidence and testimony and renders a decision called a *verdict*. In these examples, decisions are events.

Making decisions is arguably the most important job of senior executives and what they report spending most of their time doing. Thinking about decisions as events wrongly limits our perspective and keeps decision makers from becoming truly great leaders.

"The fact is decision making is not an event. It's a process, one that unfolds over weeks, months, and even years," according to David Garvin from Harvard University and Michael Roberto from Bryant University. It is a process "fraught with power plays and politics and is replete with personal nuances and institutional history; one that's rife with discussion and debate; and that requires support at all levels of the organization when it comes time for execution."

In my career, I have learned decisions are never independent. Instead, they exist in a larger structure of interconnections and dependencies, so much so that the value of any discreet decision can only be determined later, after execution. Sometimes much later. This book shows the relationship between decisions and implementation.

After all, a diagnosis for the patient marks the beginning of a recommended treatment plan. A verdict in a courtroom is followed quickly by sentencing and fines or freedom. Business decisions, likewise, lead to other decisions. The idea that a decision maker controls the outcome by making a *correct* decision is a fantasy. It is a dangerous oversimplification that keeps decisions and leaders from reaching their full potential.

Instead, we should recognize decisions are *both* finish lines and starting lines. The organizational resources necessary to support the decision overwhelmingly happen after the decision. We think of decisions as a point of convergence, but successful decisions diverge into a torrent of additional workstreams. Over time, this divergence will dwarf the work that went into assessing the choice.

The verb most associated with decisions is *made* or *making*. I think this is very telling and should inform how we think about decisions. Decisions are crafted, manufactured, designed, and implemented. Decisions aren't simply intellectual or emotional exercises. Making is an active verb filled with movement, collaboration, pushing, pulling, and smoothing. You don't make something with thought or conversation alone.

THERE ARE NO GOOD OR BAD DECISIONS
(AT LEAST NOT THE WAY YOU MIGHT THINK)

People make as many as 35,000 choices a day. All of them have the potential of being labeled *good* or *bad*, depending on the retrospective judgments of the outcomes. As we will see, big decisions are more like the "Choose Your Own Adventure" children's stories than they are a set course to success or failure.

Craig Heiser, president of Cardinal Gates, told me recently that fifteen years ago he found himself wanting to expand his channel reach. A few years earlier, he had purchased the company, which made premium baby and pet gates, and he went on the road to pitch his offering. "Petco, Babies"R"Us, Walmart, Target, you name it. If they sold gates or anything close to it, I booked a meeting." Yet, he was hitting brick wall after brick wall. He heard his price point was too high, and retailers could not make the margin they wanted. He would be ushered out the door from these meetings with the biggest retailers in the world, carrying only the promise his product would be considered for online sale.

"It was the consolation prize," he recalled. "Selling online was what they offered to those who couldn't get on the retail shelf."

At that time, "Walmart.com and Target.com didn't have the same business models, and they were happy to experiment," Heiser recounted. He jumped at the chance and began to experiment alongside them, learning more about his customers, these alternative channels, and how to build a successful business with these partners.

He quipped that Cardinal Gates was "an e-commerce player before e-comm was what it is today." Although the decision to go into online sales looks like a brilliant, long-term strategic move, Heiser is more humble. "It was just dumb luck. If they had let me on the shelves, I wouldn't have bothered." When he first faced rejection, it forced him to re-evaluate his options. He could have held out for retail space, redesigned his product portfolio to hit the lower price points, rethought his sourcing strategy, or explored other alternative channels where pet owners and parents shop. Instead, he made the decision to master online selling, which was not dumb at all.

Fast-forward to today, and this decision has given his business a resiliency other competitors do not enjoy. "Those who were just in physical retail were really damaged when companies like Babies"R"Us went out of business," he explained. "I hooked my trailer to e-comm, because it was the only one that was moving, and that has turned out to be a great decision."

"If you obsess over whether you are making the right decision, you are basically assuming the universe will reward you for one thing and punish you for another," writes Deepak Chopra, a doctor and prolific author. Heiser's decision to sell online versus in a store did not have a determined outcome. It was a series of decisions he and his colleagues made, which, in turn, made the Cardinal Gates business.

Chopra continued by saying, "The universe has no fixed agenda. Once you make any decision, it works around that decision." Circumstances lead to circumstances. Choices are "a series of possibilities that shift with each thought, feeling, and action you experience." His observation has a grounding in biology. "Look at the body," he advised. "Every significant vital sign—body temperature, heart rate, oxygen consumption, hormone level, brain activity, and so on—alters the moment you decide to do anything... decisions are signals telling your body, mind, and environment to move in a certain direction."

The same is true of our organizations. Every decision is packed with unrealized potential. That potential is unlocked only if multiple systems or functions are working together.

Why then do we grow attached to the myth of a solitary good or bad decision when the power for true business transformation lies in what happens next? Why can't we see the whole interconnected body in motion?

Perhaps we have been thinking about this all wrong.

In 1772, a colleague asked Benjamin Franklin to help him make a career choice. Franklin replied that he didn't know enough about the specifics of the job or situation to offer advice, but he did suggest a decision-making process. "Divide half of a sheet of paper by a line into two columns, writing over the one Pro and over the other Con," he said. He then advised his friend should write out all of the ideas that come to mind over the coming days. When items on either side of the line seem equal, he should cross them out, leaving only the unique items that would inform the decision. Franklin called it "moral algebra."

What is fascinating about this approach (which has clearly stood the test of time and we all have used, I am sure) is that it is just the kind of thing that limits our thinking. What if, instead of choosing to take the job or not, Franklin's friend had considered other options? Perhaps he could negotiate a short-term trial arrangement to see if he liked the new position. Perhaps he could have started his own business in the field. Perhaps not this job, but another was of interest. Or perhaps there were some things he could do in his current profession with his current employer to achieve more fulfillment.

Certainly, business leaders should avoid making decisions that can be reduced to a pro and con list. But there is a larger lesson. If this time-tested framework can lead to uninspired outcomes, what other things are we thinking about wrongly? As this example illustrates, if we are going to make what we later deem good decisions, then with thoughtful consideration and momentum-building action, we must rethink our frames.

JUDGING THE WATERS

What is the most important thing a business leader can do to make decisions with better outcomes? They can recognize what kind of decision needs to be made. They need to exercise judgment before they can exercise judgment. I contend, at the scale of an enterprise, defining the type of decision you are making is more important than the ability to make wise decisions in each case.

In a 1997 letter to shareholders, Jeff Bezos, Amazon founder and former CEO outlined the company's philosophy about decision types. At the time, they had around 250 employees and had revenue of $147.4 million dollars (a fraction of what they have today). In order to maintain what Bezos envisioned as an "invention machine," he needed to avoid "one-size-fits-all decision making."

"Some decisions are consequential and irreversible or nearly irreversible—one-way doors—and these decisions must be made methodically, carefully, slowly, with great deliberation and consultation," Bezos went on to explain. "If you walk through and don't like what you see on the other side, you can't get back to where you were before." Sometimes called *high stakes* or *strategic*, these kinds of decisions constrain your choices in the future and establish hard-to-change expectations with your customers or important stakeholders.

A quintessential example of a one-way door decision is establishing the legal structure and operations of a company. Angela Evans, a CPA who heads up a section of the tax practice as a partner at EY, described to me recently how the amount companies pay in tax is a function of how much money they profit, certainly, but perhaps more importantly, where that profit is made. You can change the legal structure and location of factories or selling organizations, but only at great expense and effort.

This explains why over one million business entities are registered in the state of Delaware, a small northeastern state measuring less than 2,000 square miles with less than one million residents. The answer is simple: there is no state tax. Similarly, places like the Cayman Islands or locations like Ireland, Switzerland, or Singapore have gained a reputation for favorable tax treatment and other business benefits.

Usually, when a company builds up a big enough business in a certain region, a one-way door decision is triggered, and Evans and others in the tax profession step in to advise. "We look at their entire supply chain and say, 'if you move to this jurisdiction, you'll get this tax rate,' or you'll get this VAT rate, and other things that will lower their overall effective tax rate," she described. "It is a combination of modeling and analysis, to balance things like higher transportation costs and import or export duties against the lower tax rates, at scale, built to anticipate their future forecasts and strategies." Their clients add to this their own analysis before the consequential one-way door decisions are made. But that analysis always relies on assumptions.

"My Dad always told me you make the best decision you can in the water you are swimming in at the time," she offered. This is certainly true of these corporate structures and investment decisions. "The current and forecasted tax and regulatory environments are the waters in which they were swimming," Evans continued. "The decision where to locate a factory isn't what generates the value. Instead, it is the execution of the plan and the assumption that circumstances won't change."

If outside factors do change, like if a country or region change their tax structure, the previous decisions may no longer be optimal and the cost of unwinding or changing the decision can be extreme. Take, for instance, the legal battles that are going on now between the European Union (EU) and large technology companies with operations in Ireland. Those companies made decisions under one tax structure only to have the EU challenge the policies, resulting in billions of dollars of contested tax liabilities. Only time will tell how the waters might change in this particular case, but it illustrates how the strategic decision to incorporate in a particular place or set up a factory is a one-way decision for most organizations.

In the Amazon shareholder letter, Bezos continued to say most decisions aren't forever choices. "They are changeable, reversible—they're two-way doors." In these cases, "If you've made a suboptimal Type 2 decision, you don't have to live with the consequences for that long. You can reopen the door and go back through." For this reason, he advises two-way door decisions can and should be made quickly by high-judgment individuals or small groups.

The key is to identify what choice you are facing and whether it's a one-way or two-way door. "As organizations get larger, there seems to be a tendency to use the heavy-weight Type 1 decision-making process on most decisions, including many Type 2 decisions," Bezos observed. "The end result of this is slowness, unthoughtful risk aversion, failure to experiment sufficiently, and consequently diminished invention."

When you are faced with a one-way door or want to pursue a high-stakes decision, even then, there are ways you can lower the risk and permanence of choices. You can turn one-way doors into two-way doors.

INSTALL HINGES: CALL IT A "PILOT"

It is very common in technology businesses to develop what serial entrepreneur Steve Blank called a "Minimum Viable Product" that can be tested with actual customers to provide data. In his book *The Lean Startup*, Eric Ries makes the claim that in our modern economy, with access to the range of technology and resources available, you can create almost any product imaginable. The question, he says, isn't "Can this product or offering be built?" The more relevant questions are "Should this product be built?>". In other words, does it solve a real and compelling customer problem that we understand well enough, and are we the ones to do it? Further, leaders should ask, "Can we build a sustainable business around this set of products and services?"

Sometimes the key to making a one-way door into a two-way door is asking, "How can we test this on a small scale?" or "What would a pilot look like?"

Nick Nelson, a brand strategist and CEO, summed it up well for his clients: "Sell First! Build later." I have been a part of pilot programs, marketing campaigns, pop-up retail shops, and internal initiatives that were the answer to this question. By time-bounding and resource-limiting a test with the goal of learning (ahead of large-scale results), you gain confidence and useful insights applicable to design thinking.

Before Zappos started an online store, founder Nick Swinmurn asked to photograph the inventory of a local shoe store. He posted the photos on the internet, promising to come back and buy the shoes at full price if a customer bought them. The result was a conviction that one could create a shoe business entirely online.

Similarly, when Bill Gross founded CarsDirect.com in 1999, he wasn't sure if customers would see value in buying cars online. This was understandable, considering customers were nervous about buying shoes. A few weeks into the project, one of the executives reported that he was speaking to Ford about getting a supply of cars. Gross responded, "We don't need to worry about getting cars. Don't worry about figuring out how to scale the business. Just test the core proposition: Will someone buy a car online?"

Thirty days later, the executive came back describing the car configurator they were building to conduct the test. Gross tried to describe what a pilot in the online car business looked like. "We're going to take that print out, drive down to the Honda Auto Mall in Monrovia, buy the car at retail, and sell it to them at cost," he said. "We're going to lose $4,000 on each car. We don't care about that. We're just trying to find out if someone will go through with it." His executive team treated the pilot like a one-way door when Gross wanted to keep it a two-way door.

On the eightieth day, Gross pushed his team to publish the website. When he came back the next morning, they had sold four cars overnight. Surprised, Gross said, "Hurry up and turn the site off! We don't want to sell any more cars." They had proven their thesis. Gross's team bought the cars and delivered them on flatbed trucks to the pioneering customers. From there, they built a business which, along with others under the parent company Internet Brands, sold to Hellman & Friedman Capital Partners and JMI Equity for $640 million in 2014, who then sold it to Kohlberg Kravis Roberts (KKR & CO LP) in 2014 for $1.1 billion.

I fell into the trap of treating two-way doors like one-way doors in an entrepreneurial effort I started in 2007. I had the idea for a crowdsourced, print-on-demand gift book business I named "Remarkable Tributes." Customers would go online and select their occasion, like a wedding anniversary, birthday, or retirement. They would send out invitations to people who would then submit pictures and text to go into the book (and a personalized website for those who wanted that). I met with some talented software designers and set about building the site.

While we were coding, I had done a few side projects for friends to test the concept. Those experiments were well-received, so I thought I had done the due diligence to know a business existed. However, in hindsight, those experiments proved that I could sell something to people I know (who loved me and wanted to support me, which is wonderful but probably not a scalable target audience). I also proved I could send a file to a supplier and get back a book. All of the other details I had hard-coded into the site around templates, editability, approvals, and user experience, I did not validate. So, I invested heavily in things I had never tested as two-way door pilots.

Instead of a full-featured website, I could have posted a page offering book services and managed a few projects with strangers via email before committing to a full web experience. I could have done more manual processes to ensure I was on the right track. It was only after making a significant investment that I fully comprehended all the things I did not know or had made assumptions about. This was a very valuable set of lessons that I have since tried to apply.

If you want to lower your risk and exposure while increasing the rate of learning, then accelerate the rate of experiments in your organization by turning one-way doors into two-way doors:

- If you want to change prices, try some short-term promotions to test the elasticity.
- If you want to change the feature of a product, offer a select group of customers a chance to try out those features in exchange for feedback.
- If you want to improve the customer experience, A/B test different designs and compare user results.
- If you want to acquire a company, consider a partnership as an opportunity to learn about the business, its leadership, and customers (and for them to learn about you). Same with entering new markets or geographies.
- If you want to start a new line of business, think about how you can start small and learn before investing more.

One of the reasons that venture capitalists manage startups with such a short cash runway is to force them to test things in small ways to validate assumptions. This is wise advice, no matter how much funding you have. It is a discipline you can force on yourself. Of course, not everything can be A/B tested, but if you could reduce the risks of decisions with thoughtful, speedy two-way door experiments, wouldn't it be worth it?

I choose the successful internet sales examples in this chapter for a reason. You come to this book believing online businesses can be successful. It's so obvious. You and the leaders featured in these stories now have the benefit of hindsight. The truth is that things are only ever obvious in hindsight. What is known in the future (when you want to achieve results) isn't known today (when you are making decisions). You can create more hindsight—exclusively for your business and at a quicker pace—by experimenting more.

YOU ARE AN EXPERIMENT
WHO MAKES EXPERIMENTS

Modo Modo Agency CEO Moira Vetter recalled that early in her career, she took too much time to learn. "When I failed, I beat myself up rather than absorb the lesson and quickly apply it." She advises leaders to put personal feelings to the side and view themselves as a project. You succeed, she said, when you "make mistakes faster and move on." Faster than the competition. Faster than your clients or customers, so that you can stay ahead of their needs.

It isn't just the clock speed that leaders should focus on. "Being first with an idea and being first with the business model and proposition that maximizes market opportunity are very different things," she explained. This is where experimentation is key.

As we will explore in this book, as people gain experience, especially those with deep technical skills in programming, marketing, or the like, they build a reputation for knowing the answers. But leaders who turn decisions into successful businesses and can influence at scale are known for asking questions. Vetter continued, "as they say, leaders are assessed on their ability to win at their core area, and CEOs are evaluated on their ability to identify and motivate the leaders." True leaders are defined not by the envelopes they open and their decisions, but by the mosaic of decision making they preside over. Day by day—until the business is built by decisions.

PRO TIPS:

- Decisions are only as good as their implementation.
- Use rigorous decision-making processes only for one-way door decisions, making the best assumptions you can at the time.
- Install hinges on as many decisions as you can—to experiment, risk less, and grow your judgment.
- Allow yourself to experiment and know your long-term success will be built through decisions and through the team.

CHAPTER 2:

A TALENT FOR DECISION MAKING

---

*"Give a good idea to a mediocre team, and they will screw it up.
Give a mediocre idea to a great team, and they will either fix
it or come up with something better.
If you get the team right, chances are that they'll get the
ideas right."*

—ED CATMULL, THE CEO OF PIXAR STUDIOS, WHO HAS
MADE BOX OFFICE HITS FROM IDEAS LIKE A LOST CLOWN
FISH TO A RAT WHO DREAMS OF BEING A FRENCH CHEF

In 2001, the first internet bubble burst, and many technology companies were failing as venture capital dried up. Reed Hastings and the team at Netflix were in crisis. "We were suddenly unable to raise the additional funds we needed to run the business, which was far from profitable," he said. "Morale in the office was low, and it was about to get lower. We had to lay off a third of our workforce."

They sorted employees into a "keepers" pile and made tough choices. There was a lot of anxiety, hand wringing, and fear that it would damage the company's culture or people would be demoralized by the changes. But what happened next was a complete shock. After the initial sting (which was a no-good-very-bad day for everyone), morale was better—much better. You'd think that with fewer people, they would accomplish less, but they were actually accomplishing more. Netflix's HR leader, Patty McCord, described the environment like a lot of people who were in love with their work. It caused Hastings to reflect.

He observed that before the layoffs, they had a mix of talent on the team. Some were exceptional and others were mildly talented. "After the layoffs, with only the most talented eighty people, we had a smaller amount of talent overall, but the amount of talent per employee was greater. Our talent *density* had increased," he said. This proved to be all the difference, not just immediately but over the long run.

The variation of talent among individuals can be dramatic, especially if the roles are *knowledge work* where expertise, judgment, and creativity are all at play. While there is a limit to how well an assembly line worker can contribute to building a product, the same isn't true of high-judgment work. A classic study conducted in 1968 by Harold Sackman, W.J. Erikson, and E.E. Grant studied the output of computer programmers and found the ratio of initial coding time between the best and worst programmers was about twenty to one. For debugging tasks, they found the best was twenty-five times better than the worst. The researchers found no relationship between a programmer's amount of experience and code quality or productivity. Work has changed dramatically since that original study, yet this *orders-of-magnitude* difference has been confirmed by other studies over decades.

I have found this to be true outside of development roles. You'd think that every salesperson in a similarly sized market, given the same product offerings, lead flow, sales tools, and training, could accomplish the same results, but that hasn't been my experience. Similarly, some marketing campaign managers can run circles around others with similar experience. Knowledge work is just like that.

The staff Netflix had retained were orders of magnitude more productive than those they had to let go. Not all employees had an equal effect on the talent equation. Not all of them could code as well, transform data into insights, could manage their time effectively, or deliver the same results with the same resources. It turns out organization design isn't checkers, where the leader with the most pieces on the board is likely to win. It's more like chess—the unique capabilities of the individuals matter, even more than the number of people.

If decisions are all about implementation, how do you develop a talent for *making* a decision right? You build the talent density of your teams.

FLYING WITH EAGLES

I saw a mug once that read, "How can I fly with eagles when I work with turkeys?" It's a perfect white elephant gift for the company holiday party, I suppose, but the snarky sentiment holds truth (as well as coffee). Motivational speaker Jim Rohn has said we are the average of the five people with whom we spend the most time. We tend to calibrate to what we experience routinely. Eagles, when put in a pen with turkeys, might forget to fly, or they might fly away.

Professors Will Felps, Terence Mitchell, and Eliza Byington with the University of New South Wales in Australia conducted a study in which groups of college students were asked to complete a team task competing for a prize. Unbeknownst to the students, some teams would include actors playing the roles of *slacker, jerk,* or *depressive pessimist.*

The effect of the bad-behaving actors on team performance was dramatic over the dozens of trials conducted. Groups with one under-performer did worse than other teams by a whopping 30 to 40 percent. You might think the effect of one team member wouldn't have changed the group dynamics, but the research was conclusive. A bad apple can spoil the barrel, just as the adage says. And if you are in charge of the barrel and tasked with maintaining talent density, then your role is to attract and retain the best apples. Staffing decisions, especially at the leadership level, are some of the most important decisions a business makes for this reason.

When you're in an environment with what Hastings calls "stunning talent," leaders can trust their teams more. They can delegate more authority: actually making more decisions faster and closer to the work. In contrast, mediocre teams sap manager energy, take attention away from top performers, and can distract companies from their customers. Look back at your own experience, and you are likely to observe the same.

Top performers attract other top performers. Friendly competition and comparison can raise the bar in the company. In contrast, less talented colleagues can pull down the quality of group discussions. Hastings observed at Netflix that "when every member is excellent, performance spirals upward as employees learn from and motivate one another."

This shows up in the judgment employees display on the job every day. Judgments that later helped Netflix become a category creator.

In contrast, keeping poor performers sends a message that you accept mediocrity or relish wasteful workarounds. It is difficult to coerce top performers to stay in those environments, especially if they must live with the decisions of mediocre team members.

If you find yourself on a team with less-than-stunning talent, you have a choice to make. You either attract more eagles to your team or fly the coop yourself. Both company leaders and individual employees have a responsibility to achieve high talent density. Start with your team. Don't let a bad apple spoil the barrel. After all, no one sets out to create a mediocre team. The stakes are too high for leadership at all levels to let that happen.

High talent density can make mediocre decisions better. Gerry Perkel, a former CEO of mine who now advises leaders with CEO International, explained it like this in a recent conversation. "You can gnash your teeth about making the perfect strategic decision, but the results may be more about the people you surround yourself with," he said. "You can be ten degrees off course on your strategy, and the right people will bring it back into alignment or make the right adjustments." In contrast, "You can have a 'perfect' strategy, and if you have the wrong people, it still won't work. Your people are what make your decisions look brilliant or not," Perkel concluded.

This is especially true of transformational decisions, like those resulting in the acquisition of a company, an investment into a new market or technology, or a strategic pivot of a business. Work begins after the decision is made. Different teams with specialized functional knowledge will manage the resulting workstreams. If you have a lot of talent density, those workstreams will have the benefit of the best talent in your organization and the best the industry has to offer. If you have mediocre leaders, you can find that your execution will fail to deliver the promise.

RISING BY OSMOSIS

Decisions are an act of creativity, as much as they are the output of a rational process. Especially for those businesses facing uncertainty, competitive pressure, and rapid technology changes (and honestly, who isn't?). Framing, investigating, considering, and choosing have more to do with imagination and courage than they often do with technical expertise. And just like other acts of creativity or genius, decisions that we in hindsight call *good* often fall prey to a dangerous myth: the lone genius myth. In this well-worn story line, the hero emerges in history with superhuman talents, free of influences or precedent, and then lightning strikes with inspiration. The finished masterpiece or the successful business is revealed to great fanfare as a finished, complete artifact.

"If you believe in the lone genius myth, creativity is an antisocial act, performed by only a few great figures—most dead men with names like Mozart, Einstein, or Picasso," said artist and author, Austin Kleon whom I had the opportunity to interview recently. "The rest of us are left to stand around and gawk in awe of their achievements."

But good business decisions don't work that way. Not at all.

You can have superhuman insight, but if you lack execution your business will never succeed. You can have a spark of inspiration, but it is highly likely you will change your mind as you learn through experimentation and from interactions with your customer. You may not even be the decision-maker for the decisions that change the course of your business and lead to success.

If you look back closely at history, many of the people who we think of as lone geniuses were actually part of "a whole scene of people who were supporting each other, looking at each other's work, copying from each other, stealing ideas, and contributing ideas," Kleon noted. From famous painters to musicians to technology investors, collaboration is more common than you think. Musician and producer Brian Eno calls this effect "senius," not genius. Even great artists benefitted from talent density in their creative communities. Consider Concord, Massachusetts, in the 1850s, which gave us literary greats Ralph Waldo Emerson, Nathaniel Hawthorne, Henry David Thoreau, and Louisa May Alcott. Or Paris, Francis in the 1920s and 30s when Gertrude Stein was rubbing elbows and buying art from Cézanne, Gauguin, Matisse, and Picasso and hosting F. Scott Fitzgerald, Ernest Hemingway, and Ezra Pound.

This idea of influence and interaction doesn't take away from the talent or accomplishment of the individuals. In the ecology of business talent, it recognizes a leader is both an artist and contributor in their own right, a conductor who orchestrates other talents, and an absorber of relevant influences in order to produce the best outcome. Kleon said we should forget about "genius and think more about how we nurture and contribute to a senius."

Who wouldn't want a senius at their workplace that brings out the best in everyone? After all, no business leader is better than the team they have assembled around them. Yet very few companies and leaders are disciplined enough to do what is necessary to build this kind of talent density. We'll talk in more detail later about how to calibrate and develop employees, but as a starting place, let's talk about how you assemble the talent in the first place.

RAISING THE BAR

Due to the variation inherent in individual performance and the teamwork effects, hiring decisions are some of the most important decisions leaders make. With every hire, they are literally making thousands of decisions, representing the employee's contribution over time.

Talent density doesn't just happen in small organizations, of course, where senior leaders can directly experience the work of all employees. There are very large organizations that strive to keep their talent density high and have lessons for all leaders on how to create mechanisms to maintain talent density as you grow.

For instance, Microsoft no longer asks their interview candidates brain teasers (why are manhole covers round? to keep them from falling in the hole, obviously), which they proved to be a poor proxy for real problem-solving skills. Each interview slot is now conducted by two people to provide a broader perspective and keep a check on unconscious bias. A final interviewer, called *As-Ap*, only participates in the interview if the others believe they should extend an offer. They and the hiring manager have to agree on the hiring decision.

Amazon has a mechanism they call the Bar Raiser program that serves a similar scaling function. A bar raiser is an interviewer, most often unrelated to the role or the group who is hiring, brought into the hiring process to be an objective third party. In my first two years at Amazon alone, I conducted over 200 interviews to learn the company's best practices and joined the bar raiser program in 2020. Amazon bar raisers lead the debriefs to ensure that every person hired is better than 50 percent of those currently in similar roles.

I have personally observed that this rigorous approach has several benefits, as it relates to achieving and maintaining high talent density:

Calibration at Scale: By design, the hiring process at Amazon (and Microsoft and other places) allows more people to participate in interviews. This provides a clear and consistent reinforcement of the culture of the company and the hiring standards. There is nothing more humbling than sitting in a debrief for a candidate you liked—or worse, someone you recommended—only to hear the panel describe in detail how they did not raise the bar. This is especially valuable in the high-growth business I was a part of, where most employees had been at the company less than two years. I have found having my employees participate in interviewing and join the Bar Raiser in Training (BRIT) program, to be a highly effective onboarding and management training tool. Calibration to organization expectations and cultural tenants is a way for the CEO and other senior leaders to participate in the hiring process without having to interview every candidate.

Intellectual Honesty: A hiring manager with open roles faces incredible pressure. I have never met a manager with an open requisition that wasn't desperate to get someone in that seat. But people who are desperate make short-sided and poor decisions. Human nature might cause them to compromise and believe that "anyone is better than no one," which isn't true. A survey by Career Builder estimates that in the US, a poor hire costs over $50,000. Senior or executive positions are much more costly. And that is before factoring in all the costs of suboptimal decision-making processes, the demotivation of your star performers, and the inefficiencies of managing poor performance. Having a bar raiser and an experienced panel of interviewers keeps the hiring manager from acting rashly and lowering the talent density.

Diversity of Insight: Hiring decisions must reflect a diversity of thought and perspective, just like any other decision being evaluated. This means having people on the interview team from different parts of the business, who look differently, who unite to provide candid feedback, and commit to making the new hire successful. Said simply, if you want diversity in your staff, you need diversity in your interview teams.

Minimizes Politics: In this process, only two people need to agree on a hiring decision: the hiring manager and the bar raiser. If the hiring manager's manager or *their* manager's manager is on the interview panel, they enter feedback like everyone else. They do not hold a veto over hiring decisions. When I interviewed with Intel and Honeywell, I ended up meeting with the general manager and the CEO respectively as a *final touch point*, which resulted in very informal conversations which I am sure shed no additional light on me or the role fit. On the other end of the spectrum, I have been a part of many hiring processes where the senior-most person's opinion weighed most heavily in the decision.

Whether or not a program with this rigor is a fit for your organization, thinking critically about your recruiting process is crucial to raising your talent density. Paul Alofs serves as the CEO and president of Princess Margaret Cancer Foundation and was asked what is the single-most-important decision any leader makes. His answer in a word: hiring.

"Hiring the right people is the critical contributor to success in any organization. Great hiring decisions drive success. Poor hiring decisions hurt financial performance, damage morale, and hurt the organization in 1,000 ways," Alofs continued. "Hire well and do well!"

FUTURE-PROOFING YOUR TALENT DENSITY

Of course, talent density is a calculation that requires the organization to know what talent they need. Netflix started off in physical DVD distribution and logistics. The skills they needed in the organization would be dramatically different after they pivoted to video streaming. When the Espoo, Finland-based manufacturer Nokia was making rubber boots in 1973, their organization looked quite different than it looked in the 1990s when they dominated the cell phone market, before selling to Microsoft in 2011.

This is why some companies insist on hiring overqualified people. Like Amazon's hiring bar, Arthur Blank, cofounder of Home Depot, talks about the advantages of hiring with head room. "This gives us two advantages," he noted. "First, they'll make better decisions along the way because they have more experience. Second, we'll keep them much longer than we might otherwise do because they will be able to grow with the role." Of course, this assumes the company and individual are both in a position to grow and that they won't be underemployed indefinitely.

As organizations develop, they may find the talent they need differs from what they have, and they need to decide whether to redeploy and upskill their employees to the new challenges or make other changes.

I have seen this play out in my career many times. In one instance, I had a solid employee who, because of a set of circumstances, was struggling to perform in their evolving role. The performance improvement plan I devised proved too much, and the employee left the company to achieve success elsewhere. This employee's immediate replacement was a very high performer. In fact, the previous employee's performance plan became the new employee's onboarding plan which made comparing results easy. The difference in productivity, effectiveness, and business outcomes was dramatic. It was another example of that *orders of magnitude* effect.

In hindsight, these observations are simple. You can see clearly how better off you are with a rock star in any key role. But at the moment, it can be very difficult to see clearly or to have the courage to act on. It is too easy for employees and leaders to recalibrate their expectations to a lower standard demonstrated by their current team, rather to maintain a high bar and continue to strive toward it. The leadership that served the company in one era or helped execute one strategy might not be right for the next. If you don't recognize that, you dilute your talent density.

Paul Noble is the founder and CEO of Activu, a systems integrator and collaboration platform software company in New Jersey. He and I caught up recently about a conversation we had years before about finding the right talent. "When our technology was mostly analog, the smartest guy in the room was the one with the most experience," he explained. "The older systems required finesse and deep troubleshooting expertise." Those who were curious and committed did well. The job required craftsmanship, technique, precision, and taste.

"But that has changed," he observed. Modern software-based systems are digital, use standard protocols and interfaces, and are designed to be configured. "Today, the smartest person in the room might be the person right out of school with the most up-to-date knowledge," Noble concluded. The type of talent that made up his staff twenty years ago might not be "orders of magnitude" contributors today unless they possess the ever-valuable skill of self-motivated learning and curiosity.

For those who are already in your organization, the situation becomes more nuanced. Jeff Weiner is the executive chairman of LinkedIn, who shepherded the company through an initial public offering (IPO) in 2011 and the acquisition by Microsoft in 2016. He said that in staffing decisions, if you wait until the performance is too far below expectations, you have done the business and the employee in question, a huge disservice. "If you have to ask yourself, or others, whether or not someone on your team is doing their job, you will likely already know the answer. They're not."

Organizations committed to implementing this kind of *fire fast* talent management should be prepared to spend more in severance, outplacement services, or working with employees to place or coach them into new roles within the organization, explained Annelle Barnett, who runs a marketing recruiting firm and produces and hosts the popular Marketing Mob podcast and webinar series. If you fire too quickly, you could "miss out on a great employee because you didn't take the time to coach them or move them to another position in the company that is a better fit for the individual," Barnett advised. If the employee is a good cultural fit and has the right attitude, you may find a different role puts their strengths to use. This is only reasonable if the person isn't in a leadership role, and you have the management capacity to invest in training. The key is to think about how this employee contributes to talent density in your organization today and in the future, not through the lens of the past.

"The least compassionate thing you can do in this situation is to leave someone incapable of doing their job in that role for too long," Weiner continued. It not only has an impact on your business outcomes, but on their self-confidence, the high performers on their teams, and they are likely "bringing that energy home to their families" as well. He concluded that "the most compassionate thing you can do in this situation is to alleviate their suffering by transitioning them out of the role as gracefully and constructively as possible."

And what is left, after your disciplined hiring processes and your courageous talent management, is the talent density you will need to make and implement great decisions.

PRO TIPS:
- Build the talent density of your teams, and don't underestimate the destructive power of poor performers.
- Build diversity into your interview teams to ensure you get the diversity you will need to help inform future decisions well.
- Know what talent you need for your business to be successful today and into the future.
- Be purposeful and deliberate about your hiring, firing, and talent development. These are the most important decisions that leaders make.

CHAPTER 3:

HOW LEADERS DECIDE

———

"Rarely are opportunities presented to you in the perfect way, in a nice little box with a yellow bow on top. Opportunities, the good ones, they're messy and confusing and hard to recognize."

—SUSAN WOJCICKI, CEO, YOUTUBE

At Amazon, I learned that ownership is an attitude, not a title.

At other companies, roles and responsibilities were codified in organization charts and signing authority. At Amazon, I saw something else entirely. I saw leaders setting a vision for teams they did not directly manage, inviting others to join in to solve a problem. I saw people without subject matter expertise leading and learning as they went. Promotions only occurred after employees were already doing the elevated job, sometimes for extended periods of time. Job titles were misleading at best and meaningless most of the time. Your mindset made the difference.

Making the most of an environment like this, or creating that environment, requires a different sense of agency. It requires a different posture to envision new programs, create new ways of working, and evangelize a customer's need so loudly in the organization as to solicit others to join in the solution. Even in more structured corporate environments, there is something powerful about being a magnetic leader, and the team others want to join.

How does one start to attract this kind of influence? By giving it away. Leaders can't encourage a larger sense of ownership if they don't let others own. Opportunities are hard to recognize at the speed at which we do business today, so it takes a lot of eyes to see around corners and to ensure the decisions are getting made and implemented.

PUSH AUTHORITY DOWN

"Those deeper in the organization have a closer proximity to the issue at hand and are more likely to have domain expertise," Balaji Krishnamurthy, a former CEO of mine who is now the chairman of Think Shift, shared with me in a recent conversation. "Those higher in the organization have a broader view of the business and can more easily see the impact of a decision across the organization." This begs the question: which is more important in decision making: proximity or breadth of perspective? "If you aren't sure who to trust with a decision, when it doubt, push it down," Krishnamurthy advises.

Sometimes unclear decision making can create bottlenecks. As you think about your responsibilities in your organization, consider these dimensions offered by Paul Rogers and Marcia Blenko for *Harvard Business Review*, which can impact your organization:

Global vs local decision making: At large companies with international footprints, there is often ambiguity about what will be done centrally versus in various regions or market segments. Who can enter new agreements for local distribution? Can regions build and source their own products? Who is responsible for demand generation? Clarity here will make the organization more relevant and nimble.

Central vs business unit or line of business: I have seen the pendulum swing back and forth in my career as different decisions and organizations are centralized then decentralized. There are pros and cons to each, but no matter the current organizational structure of your team, decision making needs to be clear. For instance, who approves brand decisions or talks to the press? Or who approves new product investments or market expansions? You might expose the organization to undue risk or miss opportunities if you aren't clear.

Function vs function: I have written extensively about the alignment of sales and marketing, but this same potential tension and partnership exist between many functions in the organization. Who gets to decide what is on the roadmap, product management or research and development? Who gets to decide how much risk is in investment decisions, finance, or marketing? Who gets to pick and implement systems, IT or business units? I have found that without clarity of charter, organizations can duplicate effort and waste resources. However, with too much rigidity, the organization can become bureaucratic or plagued by consensus decision making. Striking a balance here is key.

Inside vs outside partners: As outsourcing, joint ventures, strategic alliances, franchising, and channel partnerships (often with frenemies who collaborate in some markets and compete in others), become more common, decisions on who to involve and how these relationships are structured can slow the organization down. I have observed great ideas left unactioned because there was a lack of clarity about how this work could get done in the organization.

Ultimately delegation is an act of self-discipline from leaders. "I have asked hundreds of CEOs what happens when their team makes a decision different than their own opinion," Krishnamurthy recalled. "More often than not, they'll say 'I let them make the wrong decision and learn from it.'" Implicit in this answer is that the CEO or the senior most leader would have done the right thing, and it's a learning opportunity for their team.

"That very mindset is the mistake," he continued. It doesn't recognize the shared responsibility we all have to make decisions successful, and in addition, the leader robs themselves of something powerful. "They miss the chance to learn from the decisions their team members make," he said. Instead of saying, "Go ahead and make the decision and then you'll learn," they should say, "Go ahead and make the decisions and I'll learn."

As an example of this, Krishnamurthy references the decision to hire me back at Planar after I had left for Intel. The hiring manager, Erick Petersen, was convinced I was the right person for his leadership team. Krishnamurthy, who was CEO, thought that people who left probably had lingering reasons and wouldn't boomerang successfully. He and I are both happy to admit that he was wrong.

If you find two-way door decisions are making it into your inbox, you should work to delegate and drive faster decision making on your team. As a leader who wishes to drive with high velocity you must resist the urge to jump in and take charge or provide direction when others in your organization can and should be leading. It is a hard lesson for high achievers to learn, but anything less will hold you back. Assuming you have the right talent density, rather than jumping in on two-way door decisions of your team, the most important thing you can do is to empower them.

GIVING FREEDOM THROUGH CONSTRAINTS

Sara Fritsch joined Schoolhouse Electric & Supply Co. leading product in 2015. She was named president in 2018, bringing her deep business acumen and a quirky personal style to the company, which manufactures 80 percent of its heirloom-quality home products in the US: 60 percent in their own factory. They operate from a storefront in the industrial northwest corner of Portland, Oregon, in a brick building zoned for manufacturing, yet still convenient for customers. The factory and the retail store share this building and a common philosophy: a framework of questions for decision making that Fritsch called "filters" in our recent conversation.

Product development is a core competency of the company. "Whether we are designing the products ourselves or buying products wholesale, a process we call 'cool hunting,' we want products that are befitting our brand," Fritsch explained. They start by hiring talented tastemakers. "We have cool people in the company with highly elevated taste picking fabrics, colors, textures, and the 1,000 other decisions they make every day. But it isn't enough to hire top talent. You have to give them filters."

For Schoolhouse, these filters are a list of six or so questions people use to judge product fit. Questions around usefulness, ethical sourcing, and function in the home. "Within those filters or constraints, it is a safe space for them to be super creative," Fritsch said. "I don't have to get involved to have opinions about a throw pillow or any particular product because we agreed that pillows make sense. They are then free to make micro-decisions around fringe and zippers, looking at trends twelve to eighteen months in advance. These choices affect our brand, and they could only be well made with constraints."

Every business has constraints, whether they be financial, regulatory, creative, or the universal limitation of time. Fritsch commented that "any creative or design thinker loves and welcomes that." Researchers for the *Harvard Business Review* evaluated 145 empirical studies on the effects of constraints on creativity and innovation. They found that individuals, teams, and organizations alike benefit from a healthy dose of constraints. It is only when the constraints become too high that they stifle creativity and innovation.

"No matter what filters or framework you have in place, it is people and their choices that make the business," Fritsch continued. "In the creative space, it's the people with a honed-in aesthetic that kind of get it or push it to a new place. In the factory, we have studied lean and different workflow management styles, but it is people who layout the work. It comes down to the people and their ability to work within the framework to make decisions in the moment."

Zooming out on the day-to-day decisions, the same idea of filters applies at the corporate level.

DON'T FORGET TO CLOSE DOORS

My college alma mater, Warner Pacific University, is located right in the heart of Portland, Oregon, on the side of a dormant volcano, Mount Tabor. When Dr. Andrea Cook joined in a development role, "there were some on the board that believed being in the city was just too difficult and they had identified three different properties in the outer suburbs for a new campus, including one in Boring, Oregon," Cook recalled in a recent conversation.

"Are you kidding me?" she said to the board. "You want me to recruit students to a town called Boring?" The other proposed locations were out of town or very near other established schools. They had done a study to determine the value of the Portland campus and intended to borrow a playbook from other successful liberal arts schools. They had already assembled a task force to look into the move.

But Cook had a different vision. "I sat down and wrote a seven-page letter to reflect the first month's musings," she said. "I told them we are in trouble if we don't really transform the place." In no uncertain terms, she believed "moving the institution would kill it. The greatest opportunity we have is staying right where we are." The current campus was landlocked as the city grew up around it and lacked the facilities of other liberal arts colleges, but it was in the city and easily accessed from public transit from the corners of the metro area. The location would need to be the center of a whole round of changes that wouldn't just accept the urban location but would reflect a larger pivot "from being insular to being outward-reaching: to love our city, love our neighbors, and serve them."

The final piece of her strategy came in a meeting of area college presidents where the presenter talked about the changing demographics in the state, based on data from primary schools projected out into the future. "We saw the African-American population would grow slightly, along with the Asian population, while the white population would decline dramatically. The Hispanic population just went off the charts," she recalled. The presenter concluded with this bleak prediction for private liberal arts education in Oregon, which had historically matriculated white graduates: "You know what this means. We are all going to be competing harder for our target population that is shrinking."

Cook thought to herself, "You guys knock yourselves out." There was something so obvious on that chart everyone else was missing. Warner Pacific didn't need to compete for upper-middle-class white students, as they had in the past and as these other schools were still committing to do. They didn't need to move the campus. They were already in the center of the action in the fastest growing demographic in the state. They just needed to be themselves. In her inaugural address, when she later took over as president, she made a declaration that Warner Pacific's urban identity would become its organizing principle. To open the door to a new vision, she had to close the door on the previous options and proposals to move the school.

Today, I am proud to say students of color represent more than 60 percent of the student body. The university is the first and only four-year campus designated by the Department of Education as Hispanic serving. More than 35 percent are first-generation students, with 57 percent qualifying for government Pell Grants. A suburban campus would have prevented these results. Cook committed the school to *radical excellence*, providing a vision of what could be possible.

To make decisions great, leaders must have the courage to close doors, like Cook did when she shut down the suburban campus plans to focus on her urban vision. "Bigger doors (or those that seem bigger) are harder to close," notes famed economist Dr. Daniel Ariely. "We have an irrational compulsion to keep doors open." And at work, leaders keep options open too long as a form of procrastination.

Not all delays, of course, are the result of analysis paralysis. Sometimes what is observed as slow decision making is the result of leadership having a broader view or unique knowledge of the situations. Perhaps leaders are reluctant to change pricing or implement a reorganization because they know they are in the midst of a negotiation to sell that business division or add some new leadership in the mix. Perhaps there is more to the story. But even with that aside, leaders should know that every door they keep *open* is ambiguity they are adding to the organization. They need to be prepared to say *no* quickly to bring the focus back to the strategic priorities.

THINK LONG, ACT SHORT

"I think the word 'strategic' is such a tough concept because everyone looks at it differently," Teresa Caro told me in a recent interview. Caro is the chief marketing officer at Sagepath, a digital transformation agency. As an author and expert in customer engagement and digital marketing, she is often called upon to advise clients to think beyond a campaign or demand generation initiative to think about their business differently.

"People will often come to agencies and consultants asking for a brand refresh, asking to build a website, asking us to set them up on Pinterest or YouTube or TikTok, but often those are 'check box items'," she observes. "They forget to ask why." In a similar situation to what Dr. Cook found herself in at Warner Pacific, organizations of all types need to be reminded of their purposes to make sound decisions. Attributing the insight to her previous boss at the LUCKIE agency, Caro noted that "brands can look at their shoes instead of looking at the road ahead." They can focus on a single product launch, campaign, or project and miss the larger picture.

"It isn't just about what the product does or how many customers you can acquire in one campaign," Caro continued. "It is about how to get that person to remain loyal and become an advocate for the brand because they feel good about what they have bought, and they know what the brand represents." With this longer-term view, there is a higher likelihood of retention. Further, "when you know what problems you are really solving, you don't waste time solving the wrong problem," she added. "You also make sure you are measuring the right things, broadly enough and from a future perspective that makes sense long-term."

Businesses, especially public ones, are criticized for living quarter to quarter. However, research has shown that those businesses and business leaders who have their feet firmly on the ground and plan for the future are more likely to succeed over a longer time than those businesses that solely focus on delivering results for the present.

Caro credits lasting brands with developing the right balance. "The goal can't just be short-term sales," she said. Financial results aren't a strong enough *why* to provide direction or inspire your teams or customers. "If you look at long-standing companies like Chipotle, who you might recall had food that was literally killing people, you see continued success because they know they are bigger than their next burrito." In their case, the customers may be sold on the idea of working with farmers and having food that is grown and raised with no chemicals. Because these values permeate their organization, they sell more burritos on their way to the larger purpose.

This approach, and the focus on long-term customer experience, changes how work is done in the organization. You can't start with tactics. Caro advises clients that you don't build a TikTok campaign without thinking about the website. You don't build a website without thinking about the experience people are having with the product. You can't think of the product experience without thinking about the customer problem deeply. Tactics need to nest within the strategy you are pursuing to solve your customer's problem best. As a lean start-up advisor once wrote, "We need to fall in love with the problem, not the solution." This means giving up our role as a solution provider.

DON'T LET WHAT YOU KNOW LIMIT YOU

Leaders like to be experts. Since 1776, when economist Adam Smith described how the division of labor could drive economic progress, work has been increasingly broken into smaller and smaller tasks. When combined with technological advances, we have entered the era of hyperspecialization. In the field of marketing alone, where I have spent a lot of my career, there are hundreds of specialties. There are job titles like "video marketers" or "search engine optimization experts," which can focus people narrowly on a subset of problems. Marketers certified in particular tools are tempted to look at customer problems through the lens of the tool they know.

"A competitive labor market does do a pretty good job of channeling people into jobs that suit them," said economist Dr. Richard Thaler. "But ironically, this logic may become less compelling as we move up the managerial ladder. This is the famous Peter Principle: people keep getting promoted until they reach their level of incompetence."

This incompetence often comes because the person hasn't retooled themselves for the job they have today and holds onto past practices. Abraham Maslow, psychologist, and father of Maslow's Hierarchy of Needs researched the Law of Instrument, which is a cognitive bias that involves overreliance on familiar tools. He said in his *Psychology of Science,* "I suppose it is tempting, if the only tool you have is a hammer, to treat everything as if it were a nail." If we take Peter, who has been promoted beyond his competence, and give him Maslow's hammer, in the form of specialty knowledge, then we should not be surprised by the frequency of narrow, short-term thinking. We not only look at our shoes. We cobble them together ourselves.

Maslow's hammer has been blamed for computer programmers over-engineering solutions and falling victim to ever-increasing requirements that slow product development. Leaders limited by past success can keep companies from disrupting their industries. Individuals who were successful with a particular style of communication or leadership can find that holds them back as they get promoted. Like executive coach, Marshall Goldsmith said in his book, "What got you here, won't get you there." Perhaps it is no surprise then in high-stakes leadership we find that 84 percent of companies fail at digital transformation. All because the mental models required for success are different from what might have been successful in the past.

Of course, it's important the functional leaders know their stuff and keep up with advances in their field. They need to make sure they themselves are contributing to the talent density of the organization. Social media marketers should know about Facebook, YouTube, TikTok, and Clubhouse (and whatever might come next). Accountants should know the latest tax practices. Call center managers should know how artificial intelligence can improve customer experiences. But practitioners must be careful not to rely too heavily on their domain experience in decision making, even as they continuously learn. As they grow into leaders, they have to put that desire for expertise aside. They need to move from being the people who have the answers. Rather they need to become the people who ask the questions. Thoughtful, insightful questions allow experts to apply their expertise to the most pressing and impactful issues facing the business.

FIRST, AND IN EVERYTHING, BE USEFUL

"Good decision making doesn't end with a decision; it ends with implementation," wrote Bruce Rogers and Marcia Blenko with the consulting firm Bain & Company. "The objective shouldn't be consensus, which often becomes an obstacle to action, but buy-in."

Buy-in, true alignment, and commitment are accomplished by doing the opposite of what many experienced business leaders find natural.

They shouldn't try to be *good* at their jobs. They shouldn't try to have the answers. They need to give up a narrow focus on expertise. They should strive to be useful.

Michael Port is the author of *Book Yourself Solid* and advises clients on how to build their personal brand and their business. He told me recently about advising an author client who was nervous she would bomb her interview on *Good Morning America.*

"Just tell me how to be good," she pleaded frantically.

He replied, "You cannot be good." There was a long pause.

"Well, you don't think I am good?" she questioned nervously. That wasn't his point.

He went on to say that "You can't go into an opportunity trying to be good because that makes the opportunity about you. What you can do, however, is to go in there trying to be helpful."

This is true of interviews, book writing, and leadership. If you approach it from a spirit of servanthood, the outcomes are better. Leaders are most helpful when they don't attempt to have all the answers or do all the work. Their role is to find the right answer. In fact, great decision-makers, who have hyperspecialized expertise in various areas, can make poor leaders if they don't decide to unlearn or set their egos aside.

Leaders can pride themselves on being able to see around corners. But perceiving around an opaque corner is only possible when we empower and trust others to tell us the truth of what they see. As a leader, our job is to give meaning to the reports we are getting from others and to marshal that into focused action.

PRO TIPS:
- Delegate, delegate, delegate.
- Make sure to close doors to focus the organization on the priorities that matter.
- Set strategic priorities by focusing on *why* something is important, not just *how* or *what* will be done.
- Transcend your expertise to not have the right answer but to get the right answer.
- Seek to serve first.

CHAPTER 4:

THE HERO OF YOUR COMPANY

"When a customer enters my store, forget me. He is king."

—JOHN WANAMAKER, RETAIL MERCHANT AND A
PIONEER IN MARKETING AND ADVERTISING

Poet and civil rights activist Dr. Maya Angelou famously observed that "people will forget what you said, people will forget what you did, but people will never forget how you made them feel." As a marketer and an achievement-oriented person, it stings a little to know people might skip over my carefully crafted words and the meticulously planned actions, but I have also found this to be true, especially when it comes to customers.

For a while, I wrote for *Forbes* on the topic of sales and marketing alignment and the customer-centric enterprise. I had the privilege of interviewing dozens of business leaders across different industries. They represented very different customers. And they all emphatically agreed that they put those customers first. When I joined Amazon, whose centering leadership principle is "customer obsession," I thought I knew what that meant after decades in business. I was mistaken.

But before you skip this chapter thinking that it is all "motherhood and apple pie," I want to share some of what I have learned about customer obsession that might cast a new light on how you can rethink what it means to put the customer first in your decisions and how you can help your business arrive at the answers that will prove right.

THE HERO OF THE STORY

Donald Miller is a *New York Times* best-selling novelist and CEO of StoryBrand, a company that consults with businesses on how to tell their stories. His principle number one, which I can only imagine is the money move of his consulting practice, is this: "The customer is the hero, not your brand."

Drawing parallels between the introduction of protagonists in movies and novels, he observed that "A story starts with a hero who wants something." Along their journey, they are helped by a *guide* to assist them on their way, which is the position that our companies and our brand should take in the lives of our customers. We are all "tempted to position our brand as the hero because heroes are strong and capable and the center of attention." We want to tell people how great we are and build their trust. However, if you think about your favorite film or book, it was "the guide, not the hero, [who] is the one with the most authority," he said. Yet, "the story is rarely about the guide. The guide simply plays a role."

If you look at the websites or marketing of some market leaders known for customer-centricity, one thing likely jumps out: those brands don't explain who they are. They don't introduce the guide, before they introduce the hero. This would be like introducing Yoda before Luke Skywalker in *Star Wars*. The hero should come first.

It doesn't take much work to find lots of examples of companies elevating themselves to hero status. A medical company starts its website with, "We are a company dedicated to elevating the status quo, every day, in everything we do." This lovely copywriting is all about the guide, not the hero. It explains what the guide does every day, not what the hero is trying to accomplish.

Another company with a range of businesses puts their organization chart on the home page, inviting people to click on "advanced materials and chemicals" or "consumer." In this case, not the company, but the lines of business are playing the role of the protagonist in the story.

Another firm encourages visitors to find out how the company innovates, claiming "the future is ours to create." A bank introduces "the best checking account we've made (seriously… it's amazing)." A software company claims they are a "best-in-class B2B solution," offering a host of features. Companies are firing customers from their rightful place as the lead character of the story. It is chronic.

All of these companies innovate every day on behalf of their customers, and I am sure they would all claim to be customer-centric. Where did we go wrong?

THE CENTER OF THE STRATEGY

Companies have many choices for how they make investments and set corporate strategies. Tomes have been written about the various approaches to make these decisions. Jeff Bezos, who founded Amazon, summarized them into two categories. Taking "inventory of what you're good at and extend out from your skills," is the first approach he explained. In contrast, you can "determine what your customers need and work backward, even if it requires learning new skills."

In one approach, you find application for your current abilities by asking: "We are really good at X. What else can we do with X?" This is the approach taken when Kodak expanded from general photography into film for medical imaging X-rays in 1896 or sound motion pictures in 1929. Those extensions of their core each became successful contributors to their business. Kodak's medical business sold in 2007 for $2.35 billion in cash. Kodak is the last big supplier of motion picture film with deals in place with Disney, NBC Universal, Paramount, Sony, and Warner Bros.

Taken to extremes, this approach, which elevates skills and capabilities, can become "solutions looking for a problem." Early in the days of electroluminescent (EL) display research and development, the discovery was made that thin films could be placed on transparent substrates to create a clear display. Glass would light up with images or readout information. With other advantages around viewing angle, unique shapes, and reliability, these displays were a solution in search of a problem when I worked at Planar.

Eventually, the technology found some success in transportation for dashboard read-outs or telescopic sight applications. This EL business was sold by Planar to the Finnish company Beneq in 2012 for $6.5 million dollars, well below the SciFi vision for how transparent displays could become ubiquitous and transform the world. Examples of this variety clutter business annuals. New inventions often lack immediate application and search for markets that never fully materialize. Innovations fail when they do not well-serve the hero.

When describing the different approaches, Bezos warned companies that use this approach would "never be driven to develop fresh skills," which means "eventually, the existing skills will become outmoded." Deep expertise in analog film or thin-film electroluminescent display technologies have diminishing market value, as these examples illustrate.

The alternative—"working backward from the customer"—has an opposite effect, Bezos concluded. It demands the company "acquire new competencies and exercise new muscles, never mind how uncomfortable and awkward feeling those first steps might be." This is the approach used by Amazon to enter businesses and markets far beyond their initial start as an online bookseller, including electronics and cloud computing services.

The customer gives your business a sustainable and higher source of enterprise value and profit than any research and development investment you could find on the balance sheet. In my experience, the cost of acquiring a new customer is much higher than nurturing an existing customer. And our finance partners will tell you those customers are more profitable. According to research by Bain & Company, among their financial services clients, a 5 percent increase in customer retention produces more than a 25 percent increase in profit. Existing customers tend to buy more, consume less operating costs, may pay a premium to avoid switching, and will refer customers to your company.

Yet, our strategy planning can value nurturing a customer with new offerings less than entering new markets and having to find new customers. We overvalue the investments we have made in technology and undervalue the investments we make in customers. This affects how we approach product development.

THE IMPORTANCE OF CUSTOMER DEVELOPMENT

"Every company has some methodology for Product Development, launch, and life-cycle management," observed Steven Blank, the entrepreneur and Silicon Valley investor and advisor. "Yet at the end of the day, even with all these procedures, the embarrassing fact is that nine out of ten new products are failures." In spite of the rigorous engineering checkpoints, market sizing exercises, rigorous sales estimates, the creation of market requirements documents, and prioritized product features, something is still missing.

"The difference between the winners and the losers is simple," Blank continued. "Products developed with senior management out in front of customers, early and often, win." In contrast, products handed off to a sales and marketing organization where customers have only been tangentially involved in the new development process lose. "It's that simple," he concluded.

To address the blindness leaders often have about how hard it is to attract and retain customers, Blank advocates for Customer Development activities to happen alongside Product Development. It starts with a series of hypotheses, each covering different aspects of the product and go-to-market activities. In this process, customers are discovered, validated, and developed, just like proof of concepts or prototypes lead to finished, sellable products.

At Planar, we had an interest in entering the high-growth and very promising LED (light-emitting diode) video wall business. The well-established technology in digital billboards and scoreboards was getting more sophisticated, allowing finer resolution at lower prices. For the first time, this opened the door for indoor applications of the technology. China had invested heavily, and new entrants from Asia were starting to disrupt the mature display and audiovisual markets that Planar served.

Me and our product team knew if we led with the same specs as everyone else, it would be a race to the bottom for price and availability. Although it was not a mature category (yet), we could see what authors W. Chan Kim and Renée Mauborgne called a "red ocean" approaching: an undifferentiated market where supply exceeds demand and competition would be fierce.

In their book, *Blue Ocean Strategy*, they tell the story of how Cirque du Soleil is a circus but is unlike other circuses. They don't have any animals in the act. They serve wine, not unshelled peanuts. They appeal to adults, not children. As a result of these important differences, the Montreal, Canada-based company is the largest contemporary circus producer in the world and are seen by more than 150 million spectators. Ringling Bros. and Barnum & Bailey took more than a hundred years to attain what Cirque Du Soleil achieved in twenty. Because they are different, they can charge a premium for an elevated entertainment experience. Planar needed the same differentiated niche.

To get close to the customer problem, we hosted a series of customer meetings, bringing in those who had extensive experience specifying and installing LED video walls. In discussions with those who knew best and by observing ourselves the challenges with installation and design, we gained insights and our path forward.

We observed that the existing LED video wall tile suppliers were electronics companies at their heart. They were happily cranking out LED tiles, which looked like circuit boards, from their factories. They bragged about their production volume and innovated only on one dimension, which was pixel pitch (a measurement of pixel size). Most interestingly, the incumbents had built their domestic business in locales famous for cheap labor. The tiles were expensive, especially those fine pixel pitch varieties for indoor use, but the labor to install them was inexpensive. They could supply the tiles and throw bodies at all the other related issues, like set-up complexity. This, however, did not solve the customer's problem.

Up until this point, LED tiles were hung from a scaffolding-style structure that was sourced locally and assembled on site. This led to labor-intensive installations, wasted space, and added expense. Our approach would be different. The need was to put more pixels up in the highest quality, fastest, and most cost-effective way possible directly onto the wall.

I was leading marketing when we launched the Planar® DirectLight™ in 2015 with a super-thin mounting system and unique servicing options. It received widespread industry recognition, winning awards from leading industry publications. Our continued customer focus sent individuals from research and development and product management out to assist with and observe early installations, continuing to iterate and developing a backlog of new features that kept the product in the forefront.

We released it with a set of sales enablement tools, like a video wall calculator, that allowed for easy specification and visualization. Innovation continued on the software side as we released new tools to help our channel partners and their customers win more business faster. We secured a copyright on these tools and kept competitors from copying our unique approach. Taking the position of a guide, we led customers to better outcomes for their businesses, putting our customers in their rightful place as the hero.

We were competing in a different circus than others because we took the time to understand what customers needed to become successful. It was insight-driven innovation: the only kind that pays.

THE HERO'S JOURNEY

The late author and Harvard professor Clayton Christensen and his collaborators proposed the Theory of Jobs. In it, he observed that "when you buy a product, we essentially 'hire' something to get a job done. If it does the job well, when we are confronted with the same job, we hire that same product again," he explained. And alternatively, "if the product does a crummy job, we 'fire' it and look around for something else we might hire to solve the problem."

Using this approach through the lens of a hero's journey, we see that our hero, our customer, is trying to accomplish something. A job is the "progress they are trying to make in a particular circumstance." It is not a product. It is not the solution. It isn't just the *problem* they face, although that might be a part of it, or a barrier to their success. Their desire for progress past problems leads them to need a guide, which is the role that we must play.

Founder Jack Dorsey was running Square from his apartment in the early days. His window overlooked a plaza where Cheri Mims ran a flower cart. The founders struck up a conversation with her and asked if she'd be interested in taking credit cards. She was skeptical at first, but remembered she had just missed a sale from a customer who didn't have any cash on hand. Mims became one of Square's first customers ringing up a sale that afternoon.

Square is a technology company at its core. They figured out how to pass credit card payment processing information via the 3.5 mm. headphone jack on a phone or tablet, enabling a whole new business model and customer experience for solopreneurs, shopkeepers, craft fair booth personnel, and coffee baristas around the world. These customers had access to credit card payment processing solutions. But they were arduous and slow. In fact, it took Square longer to get approval from Visa and Mastercard to accept a swipe than it did to create a prototype for the entire payment system (no wonder Visa went on to be an investor). It wasn't a technology problem they were solving, per se. It was one of convenience and access.

Channeling the needs of their customers, they wanted to sell flowers, not payment solutions. It needed to be easy.

"Our sign-up process takes two minutes," Dorsey recalled. "You download an app, put in your name and address, answer three security questions, link your bank account, and you're done." Square wasn't the brainchild of experts from the financial industry. Dorsey had just come off founding Twitter. In 2012, they had fewer than five people in a company of 250 who had worked in the financial industry. "So our approach is to engineer and create and build what we want to see," he explained. Now you see their payment systems everywhere.

They disrupted the traditional cash register and payment processing industries by making a flower vendor the hero of the story, not because they had skills in financial services products. It proved more important to put the customer first. Cheryl Mims was on stage when the company went public in 2015.

I have a worn and tattered first edition of J.C. Penney's business memoir on my shelf. It was originally published in 1950 (with a retail price of $2.75, according to the book jacket). Raised on a farm, J.C. was given entrepreneurial license and a strict religious upbringing. His first employer was a general store in Denver, and he established his own store in 1902 in Kemmerer, Wyoming, which bore the name the "Golden Rule," the colloquial title for the aphorism "do unto others as you'd have them do unto you."

When describing the growth of what would become the J.C. Penney department store chain, he says that the Golden Rule of business is to put the customer first. This isn't the "customer is always right" because that is clearly not true and may not even be relevant. Treating people fairly and in good conscience allows you to advocate for them, even when they aren't in the room. It's about knowing the job they are hiring you to do and whether you are the best to solve that problem. It's about making them the hero of the story and letting that drive your decisions.

PRO TIPS:
- Don't try to be the hero. That is your customer's role.
- Beware when you pursue skills-forward strategies.
- Make sure to invest in customer development.
- Remember why your customers are hiring your product or service in the first place. Understand the problem you are solving. This will help ground all of your subsequent decisions.

CHAPTER 5:

YOUR GUIDE TO BEING A GUIDE

———

"People don't simply buy products or services; they pull them into their lives to make progress."

—CLAYTON CHRISTENSEN, AUTHOR AND PROFESSOR

In the Nancy Meyer romantic comedy, *The Holiday*, the character Iris, played by Kate Winslet, is visiting Los Angeles and meets an elderly Hollywood screenwriter, Arthur, played by Eli Wallach. In the course of their friendship, she shares some of the relationship challenges she faces, and he makes an observation.

"Iris," he tells her, "in the movies, we have leading ladies, and we have the best friend. You, I can tell, are a leading lady, but for some reason, you're behaving like the best friend."

She replies to him, "You're so right. You're supposed to be the leading lady of your own life."

As we discussed in the last chapter, the leading character of your business is your customer. Your job is to be their best friend. Despite what you see in the movies, being the guide on the side is harder than it looks. One must demonstrate customer obsession in all decisions to remain the guide.

PRACTICING BEING A GUIDE

Nancy Wang is the head of Data Protection Services at Amazon Web Services (AWS). She holds four patents and a host of professional accomplishments at Rubrik, Google, and the US Intelligence Community. She is also the CEO and founder of Advancing Women in Technology (or AWIT, formerly Advancing Women in Product). She uses a framework to identify the needs of her customers, especially in the context of problem-solving.

She asks three questions:

1. Why is this a problem? Is it a need or a want of our customers?
2. Why am I the specific person or group best positioned to solve this problem?
3. Why do I think the solution will be successful in solving the need?

When she applied these questions to the founding of AWIT, she found her strategic purpose. Starting with the first question, she found there were organizations focused on building a pipeline of women for roles in technology, but none focused on professionals like her.

"Great organizations are out there like Girls Who Code, Black Girls Code, and the like," she recalled. "My thought was that there wasn't really a community dedicated to mid-career professionals." Organizations like Grace Hopper focuses on early careers. Built by Girls or Girls, Inc. focus on students.

"These other organizations help people find their first internship or get their foot in the door with a nice corporate brand, but no one ever tells those who are now a people manager or a senior product manager or senior engineer, how to be an executive," Wang explained. She saw a hole in the market for herself and others who wanted to find an executive boot camp or community. Mid-career professionals did not want to be bombarded with people looking for jobs but wanted to talk to their peers about strategy, management philosophy, and how to build their brands. "There was a need that was not being fulfilled," she observed.

Wang then asked if she was best positioned to solve it. "I am one of them," she concluded. That said, she had no experience building an industry association, but she did not let that deter her. She didn't propose a skills-forward strategy but rather knew she had uncovered a durable customer need, which is much more valuable. As we have discussed before, a durable customer need transcends any particular solution and is reflective of treating the customer as the hero.

In fact, when asking if she was the one to solve the need, she made her lack of experience an advantage.

"I am not a professional nonprofit person," she added. "The first thing that captures sponsors' attention is that I have a full-time job," she added. Investment goes right back into the community. "I think that catches their attention because there is an altruistic or intrinsic sort of motivation behind me doing AWIT. I am uniquely positioned to solve that gap because I'm one of the constituents that is a part of the community."

And the final question, why will it be successful?

"I want to build a self-sustaining community that attracts new members and provides value," Wang explained. "We want every member we collect into our community to fit the profile and know that we are making a true impact." This includes bringing new value to the customer, like how in 2020, she collaborated with other leaders to create a self-paced course on product management published through Coursera. It has been a process of exploration, experimentation, and discovery as she has ensured AWIT is the right organization to solve her members' needs.

CONSTANTLY DISCOVERING THE CUSTOMER

Wang's experience echoes a common pattern in organizations that strive for customer obsession. "The most successful entrepreneurs don't begin with brilliant ideas," writes Peter Sims, a professor at Stanford, corporate advisor, and author. "They discover them." This doesn't mean entrepreneurs don't have amazing ideas. It means even those with promise are made better along the way. This is true of decision-making leaders at every level. You continually discover customers' needs through curiosity.

As an example, "Google founders Larry Page and Sergey Brin didn't set out to create the fastest growing start-up in history," Sims continued. They didn't set out to revolutionize the way we search for information on the web or become a household brand name. "Their first goal, as collaborators on the Stanford Digital Library Project, was to solve a much smaller problem: how to prioritize library searches online," Sims recalls. It was actually Page and Brin's landlord, Susan Wojcicki, who rented her Menlo Park, California garage to the duo, who eventually helped the company create its two biggest revenue streams.

"My smartest move was joining Google," Wojcicki said about leaving Intel to become Google's sixteenth employee and first marketing manager. In 2003, she suggested that Google's ad offerings not only be available in search but also on websites and blogs across the internet. The product became known as AdSense, now Google Ads. "If we show ads that no one wants to see, we don't generate revenue," she explained, demonstrating how Google plays a supportive role. "The question is: 'how do we deliver the most perfect ad for every query?'," she asked. "It has to be user-driven, and it has to be useful and relevant." The business model of pay-per-click advertising helps ensure that customers remain the leading lady.

INTERMEDIARY HEROES OR SUPPORTING ACTORS?

In 2007, Planar acquired Runco International, a home cinema front-projection video company based in Union City, California, for $36.8 million to extend our specialty solutions strategy. Video products, under the Runco and Vidikron brands, were sold to specialty value-added resellers affiliated to the Custom Electronics and Design Association (CEDIA). The business was served by manufacturer's representatives domestically and specialty distributors elsewhere calling on these local dealers. These channel partners acted as extension of the sales force. There was hardly any direct-to-consumer advertising or promotion.

Runco dealers already had relationships with high-networth individuals in their local communities. The business grew through word of mouth and the recommendation of these trusted advisors. As a result, Runco thought of the dealers as their customers. Each dealer represented independent demand for the products and could direct that demand to any brand they recommended to their clients. The Runco brand itself was like a club that the industry wanted to join.

It was not uncommon for celebrities or business leaders to fly into our major trade show for a VIP demonstration, which might be the closest to the actual customer that Runco leadership ever came. The dealer was Runco's customer, and they obsessed over what the channel needed.

When customer and channel objectives align, power and simplicity drive the arrangement. But when needs diverge, taking the side of the dealers proved to be short-sided. For instance, in the late early 2000s, dealers appreciated high-end items to sell. Runco had video projectors that retailed from $5,000 to well over $150,000. The dealer made money as a percentage of the sale. We were told that a higher performance and more expensive projector was always a good idea.

At the time of the acquisition, Runco faced two other market trends: 1) the start of a recession that squeezed the net worth of our dealer's clients and 2) the launch of better, less expensive flat-panel television technologies. Before long, the customers who had previously valued having a home cinema of their own and were willing to spend handsomely for the privilege found mixed-use spaces with flat-panel TVs more conducive to their lifestyles and preferences. They went from paying tens of thousands of dollars for high-quality video to paying thousands or less, often cutting out the high-touch dealer channels entirely.

Based on feedback from our dealers, who were looking for ways to stay in the premium end of the market, we created a product that was lauded the "Ferrari" of 3D video. It attracted industry fanfare but lackluster customer demand. A few short years later, we were phasing out not only these new products but the whole Runco line-up. After decades of the business making decisions with the dealers as the hero, we learned that both Runco and our channel partners were the guide on the side. There were other issues at play as well, which would make a great business case study. In the end, the acquisition of Runco by Planar never did quite return the synergies and opportunities that were in the original investment prospectus.

This taught me some important lessons about really understanding the customer and the role of the channels that I have since applied. If you sell through intermediaries, never forget that the end customer is the hero. Customer needs and loyalty must take precedence. No business should forget that channel partners are in place to serve the end customer (with what we hope is better service, availability, consultation, and corollary products integrated into a solution) and to serve the brand (with scale and capabilities to better serve the end customer). Take care that no one in the value chain loses sight of the customer's "job to be done."

CAN YOU BE THE HERO AND THE GUIDE?

In 2006, I had contacted the support team at 37Signals, who produced the popular Basecamp project management tool with a new idea. I suggested to them that they develop a new interactive, collaborative scheduling service. The website would allow a person to set up a calendar of events and invite people to RSVP to specific appointment times.

Let's say a hair studio wanted to use a tool like this to accept online appointments. I thought this would be cool for a variety of their small business customers, like business consultants or sales teams wishing to make an appointment. Further, I knew that I could use it right away for a community project of my own. We know now that I was envisioning something like today's Calendly, but in 2006, this didn't exist.

I sent the idea to them in some detail. The response was surprising. I thought that I would get a "thank you and we appreciate your idea" form email, and that would be that. Or better yet, an offer to collaborate to develop and test something new. Instead, I got a personal email back from Jason Fried, the founder and CEO at 37Signals, that read, "We will not be building the software you suggested. We only build things we can use, and we wouldn't use this."

Needless to say, I was a little taken aback. I'm not proud to say I sent them back an equally curt response saying how unfortunate it was that they would not be taking action on this and that I would have scheduled time to talk with them in more detail about the idea, but sadly they don't use scheduling software. But the whole thing got me thinking.

37Signals is a company that was, and is, very well-respected and builds great tools. They got a suggestion, from a current customer, for what would be a great product (in my humble opinion), and they said, "no." It wasn't something they were passionate about. It didn't fit into their vision of who uses their tools and why.

Although their response to me could have been a bit more respectful, I can see and appreciate their point. If they poured their resources into making Basecamp and other tools I used better, then I couldn't really complain. Instead, I posted the idea on a blog and hoped that someone would build it. And because it was a reasonable "job to be done" for more than just me, someone *did* build it. Calendly was recently valued at $3 billion.

If we want to put our customers first in our decision making, should you consider yourself a representative of your customer or not? Nancy Wang considered herself a customer of AWIT and struck a chord. Jason Fried from Basecamp didn't and potentially missed out. When Mark Zuckerberg started Facebook, he was just trying to connect people at his college and a few other schools. It was a need he experienced personally. When he looked around on the internet, he found services for finding music, news, information, but you "couldn't find and connect with people that you cared about," Zuckerberg said in an interview. His instincts were right. His own desire to use the product was representative of others.

That isn't always the case. In an interview with Charlie Rose in 2000, Jeff Bezos was asked what was not going to be successfully sold on the internet. He replied, "Evening gowns. I don't think evening gowns are going to do well online." Good thing the Rent the Runway founders didn't hear that interview.

In 2008, Harvard student Jenn Hyman watched her sister shell out $2,000 for a designer dress to wear for a wedding and thought wouldn't it be better if she could have rented it. The next day, she and friend Jenny Fleiss cold-called designer Diane von Furstenberg and set up a meeting. They worked diligently to create a site, testing the ideas in pop-up events, and always asked themselves whether or not it would appeal to them personally. Rent the Runway raised capital on a $1 billion valuation. They now have five million subscribers and are the world's largest dry cleaner. This is a business capability they did not set out to build, but it was required to solve their customers' problems.

I believe being your own customer is a great way to capture passion and get others on board. It's like those old Remington ads from the late 70s with president and CEO, Victor Kiam exclaiming, "I liked the shaver so much, I bought the company."

I do think it requires a great deal of discipline and self-awareness, however. You might like the product more than others due to a number of factors, not the least of which being it was your idea. It is important to deeply understand the job that *you* are hiring the product or service to do, that it won't do for others. Kaim might have liked his shave, but he probably also enjoyed the profits that the shaver brought him after he bought the company in leveraged buy-out and turned it around. No other customer would have that experience of an owner. You must be clear about how you are like your target customers and how you are different.

Inventors must be sure they aren't hiring the product to stroke their ego, to confirm their brilliance, or impress their friends, as other customers would not have those benefits. I admire leaders who love their product and can still seek out disconfirming feedback about its features and benefits to make it better. Leaders must always seek to have their assumptions, or their own experiences, disproved with new data or insights.

FOCUS ON CUSTOMERS

Ben Silbermann and his partners, Evan Sharp and Paul Sciarra, founded what they dubbed "the world's catalog of ideas," a mobile app and website called Pinterest. Silbermann isn't an engineer or programmer. As a kid who liked leaves and bugs, the idea of an online collection of imagery was appealing and a business was born. Silbermann's wife came up with the brand name Pinterest over a Thanksgiving dinner.

From the start, they obsessed about the community. "I personally wrote to the first five or seven thousand people who used the site asking them what they thought about it," Silbermann recalled. "It is hard to know what was helpful or not helpful," looking back on those early days. "We wanted to build something we were really proud of. Something that was beautiful."

The business started small and remained that way. "We were stealth but didn't mean to be stealth," he joked. "There is a lot of really good writing about start-ups about being diligent on data and iterating really quickly on things if the early tape doesn't work out," he continued. If early results don't match expectations, some are quick to pivot. "I think that is really good advice, actually, but we didn't have any resources to do that." Instead, they stayed on the path. They continued to believe in their idea and could only afford the one experiment.

They didn't focus on traditional early technology adopters, as is common for social media or tech companies. They figured that all customers had nice enough phones and internet connections. They all had access to app stores, which Silbermann called "the biggest distribution channels in the world." They could go directly to their customers, so they could skip the technology early adopters. Unlike other start-ups who sought out as much publicity and opportunities for thought leadership as possible, Silberman recalled they "never called up TechCrunch or Mashable to launch."

What they lacked in glossy press coverage or market data, they made up for with built-in direct customer interactions. "We had a lot of confidence that early people that used it really liked it," Silbermann continued. "They had heard about it from someone they cared about, and they were using it a lot in the core. The core features of the site that exist today were there from the beginning." This is in no small part due to the thousands of personal connections the team made to early customers to inform what was appealing and useful.

Might it have been different if they had pivoted their business when the early success was slow, looked to disrupt an existing category, or have been more aggressive in their promotion to early adopters? One can never know. As Silbermann noted, you can't run A/B tests on those decisions. Instead, they stayed true to the product they loved and now have 335 million people who use Pinterest each month, and over 200 billion (yes, that is billions with a B) pins have been saved on their platform. Pinterest is now the third-largest social network in the US and the 10th most relevant brand, according to the Prophet Brand Relevance Index alongside Apple, Disney, Pixar, and Spotify. And now the press calls them.

In contrast, Alexander Hamilton, American founding father and first Secretary of the Treasury, published extensively. In less than a year, between 1787 and 1788, he published fifty-one public essays defending the Constitution, part of a series called *The Federalist Papers*. In these papers, Hamilton was the guide to help his customers, the citizens of the new United States of America, understand the importance of a Federal Government and Constitution. In the hit Broadway musical, *Hamilton*, a recurring theme is this idea that no matter how heroically you live, how much you accomplish in a short amount of time, or how prolifically you write, you have no control over the story told about you. Thus is the fate of a guide. This is true of your brand as well. It's about how it makes others feel: while you are around to lead the team or company and beyond. Everyone, it seems, is part of a larger story.

You could have the best publicist or public relations agency who can help keep the news sentiment trending toward positive. Yet the ultimate story about your company won't come from the press releases you issue. The decisions you make won't be judged by your colleagues or those close to the work. Your customers will determine if your decisions provided them real useful solutions and reflected true empathy of their needs. If you are playing the role of the guide and not trying to be the hero, your reward will be longevity and loyalty. Your decisions will lead to better, more sustained, outcomes if you advocate for your customers.

PRO TIPS:

- Fall in love with the customer and their problem.
- Relate personally, if you can. Remain disciplined to how you are like and unlike your customer.
- Don't accept intermediaries (channel partners or the press) to represent the customer.
- Stay in your role as the guide on the side.

CHAPTER 6:

WRITING STRATEGY

———

"You can make anything by writing."

—C.S. LEWIS, WRITER, SCHOLAR, AND LAY THEOLOGIAN
WHO CREATED THE WORLD OF NARNIA

I have always been a word person. My go-to strategic planning tool is the aptly named Microsoft Word (or, more recently Quip, OneNote, or other tools). I always thought the suite of applications in Microsoft Office was a bit of a personality test. We once had a financial controller who would make his presentations in Excel. I have seen sales executives take meeting notes in PowerPoint. I am sure you have observed the same. But beyond personal style preferences, there is a strong business case for developing your organization into writers. The research and my experience would contend that writing leads to well-made decisions and companies.

WHEN PRESENTATIONS FAIL

I once called on some executives at Evernote, the Silicon Valley tech company who created a note-taking app now used by 225 million users. I had used their software for a while to capture ideas for marketing campaigns, blog posts, and other things, and I thought we could do business together. I don't remember much about the meeting other than these folks *hated* PowerPoint. I mean, they loathed it. One person went as far as to say that PowerPoint—literally the .ppt format—was responsible for starting wars that resulted in mass-scale death. I walked away from that conversation, convinced it was hyperbole, but it stuck with me and came back to mind years later.

We used PowerPoint to make proposals and to provide scaffolding for discussions at Planar and Intel. Like many business leaders, I was raised on PPT. That didn't prepare me for what I experienced later in my career at Honeywell. No internal meeting, however informal, was complete without a deck. And what was on slides went largely uncontested in the meetings. There was an etiquette and culture around presentations that kept people making them and listening passively to them in the meetings, and then getting work done around them.

I am certain my experience was not unique. Many organizations run in this way with impactful, multi-billion-dollar decisions made via PowerPoint or Keynote presentations. Blame it on short attention spans, more complex businesses, an emphasis on design, or more project-based education in schools, but I have observed leaders holding onto what is now a dated and ill-fitting tool for the task of decision making.

Dan Lovallo, a professor at the University of Sydney, and Olivier Sibony, who was a director at McKinsey & Company investigated 1,048 business decisions for process, including tools like presentations, and the outcomes of those decisions.

They found that the process used to make decisions mattered more than the strategic analysis by a factor of six.

"Imagine walking into a courtroom where the trial consists of a prosecutor presenting PowerPoint slides," they said to illustrate their findings. In twenty compelling charts, the prosecution would demonstrate why the defendant is guilty. The judge then would challenge some of the facts of the presentation, asks some clarifying questions, and ask the prosecutor to go back to slide seven so that they can comment on other cases they have seen with the same evidence. The prosecutor, prepared with speaker notes, would have a good answer to every objection. After this short process, the judge would decide a guilty verdict, and the accused would receive sentencing. "That wouldn't be due process, right?" the authors asked. "So, if you would find this process shocking in a courtroom, why is it acceptable when you make an investment decision?"

This illustration might be a wild oversimplification, but the scenario is common across businesses and organizations; even military operations, of which those employees at Evernote were so critical. One team argues one side of an issue. The team has a choice of what points it wants to make and how it wants to make them. The pace of the presentation and the level of rigor in the analysis is up to the speaker. Natural charisma or factors not presented or discussed can sway the decision. And the final decision maker, often a business leader or a committee, is both the challenger and the ultimate judge. Not surprisingly, this leads to poor decisions and frankly even poorer execution, as Lovallo and Sibony's research indicated.

There has to be a better way to make informed and thoughtful decisions.

WRITING AS STRATEGY

Imagine that years ago, a progressive leader was sitting captive in a conference room in a PowerPoint lecture disguised as a meeting. Whenever someone asked a question, the presenter read from their speaker notes, which they had printed out for their own reference. Exasperated, the leader asked for a break in the meeting, during which time the presenter was asked to make copies of his speaker notes for everyone in the room, and when they returned, they would all read all the presentation, including all the detailed notes and backup data, and only then they would have a discussion.

I am told that is what happened at Amazon. Perhaps you have read the headlines that Jeff Bezos had banned PowerPoint. That wasn't completely true. During my time at Amazon, we used presentations for customer meetings and event keynotes. We certainly didn't use it for day-to-day decision making. You could always tell the newbies or those not calibrated to the culture: They brought PowerPoint to internal meetings.

Meetings at Amazon begin with an all-word document which is shared and read in silence by everyone in attendance. I mean, hear-a-pin-drop silence. Notes are scribbled in the margins or comments published in a shared electronic document. Once everyone has gotten through the document, then the "presenter" or author asks for comments and observations, and a discussion begins.

The documents themselves are also peculiar. First off, they are short. A common format is the PR/FAQ (a fictional press release and a set of frequently asked questions describing a new proposal or idea), which should be one page, with backup appendices. It is the center of Amazon's famed *Working Backwards* process. Even annual strategy documents have a six-page limit. Most narratives I wrote and read were in the two-page range.

These narratives can only be words. No charts, no graphs, and no bullet points. Backup data, best presented in charts or in a table, can be in appendices, but the author cannot assume that the readers will read them. They are there for reference, not to direct the discussion. The relevant data to inform decisions needs to be pulled into the main document. The narrative must be self-explanatory and not leave conclusions up to the reader, as charts and raw data often do.

Increasingly other companies are embracing this writing culture. I understand Steve Jobs, the cofounder of Apple, hated PowerPoint. I hear Elon Musk, founder of Tesla, and Mark Cuban, the investor and Shark Tank judge, won't sit through traditional presentations.

That said, I know this writing approach has its critics. It certainly requires learning (and unlearning of past practices). It requires calibration to get everyone reliant upon this approach. It certainly uses different muscles than PowerPoint presentations and forces everyone in the company to be a better writer and reader. It is a big change for most employees. It seemed every new employee was at first surprised or resistant. However, getting on board was not optional at Amazon.

The initial curiosity I experienced when joining Amazon has been replaced by conviction. The discipline of writing and sharing feedback on that writing leads to better outcomes for reasons I outline below:

Writing is clarifying: Shane Parrish, the former intelligence agent, turned author and consultant, said, "Writing is often the process by which you realize that you do not understand what you are talking about." The only other thing that comes close is trying to execute. And writing is an easier, faster, and cheaper way to test your idea.

For this reason, the writing should begin in the earliest stages of an idea. Working backward from what customers would care about, the author should start with the *why*, as Teresa Caro suggested, and some of the questions that Nancy Wang proposed in the last chapter. You then write (and rewrite!) to clarify the value proposition. You write to position the offering. You write to coalesce all the ideas into a cohesive statement. Before you invest further time and energy, writing makes sure it is something that will make a difference for customers.

Jeff Bezos once told Charlie Rose that "When you have to write your ideas out in complete sentences and complete paragraphs, it forces a deeper clarity of thinking." Good writing—free from poor grammar or unnecessary jargon which obscures meaning—makes us better strategists and decision makers. In the same way that writing out step-by-step proofs in your sophomore geometry class made you a more logical thinker who could bring others along on your journey to the answer.

Brevity is strategy: Blaise Pascal, the French mathematician and philosopher, wrote in a letter in 1657, "I have made this longer than usual because I have not had time to make it shorter." Anyone who has written before knows that writing (or saying) a lot of words quickly can come easily. Perhaps a bit too easily. What we write can be filled with unnecessary tangents that can distract us from the real problem we are solving. In contrast, if you have to write concisely and clearly for an audience—especially one not necessarily familiar with all the nuances and details of the topic—it forces you to prioritize, to get to the point, and to make every word count. This curation is the essence of strategy.

Like a museum director deciding what to show to tell a story or elicit a feeling, strategy is an act of saying "yes" and "no." It is opening doors and closing them. Writing a coherent document takes more time than throwing bullets into a presentation, and that depth of thinking shows in the resulting decisions. The ultimate compliment for a document at Amazon was to call it "tight." That said, you can waste time and slow down decision making by trying to be perfect. Like any act of strategy or analysis, it must be balanced with speed.

Documents go deeper: "PowerPoint has clearly decreased the quality of information provided to the decision maker," said retired Marine Corps officer T.X. Hammes. He recounts that instead of wasting time on building complex illustrations, we should put more thought into preparing the analysis. In a meeting he attended and presided over, he observed how a decision maker "sits through a twenty-minute Power-Point presentation followed by a five-minute discussion and then is expected to make a decision." In this case, it was a one-way door investment decision or something impacting human life. That ratio seems off and is unfair to the decision maker.

Documents are invitations: In corporate cultures that heavily rely on PowerPoint, decisions favor the charismatic. The great presenter, who can excite the audience and think on their feet, can dominate strategy conversations. As a high-energy person, I have benefited from this inherent bias. In contrast, when a document has to stand on its own merit, ideas can come from anywhere. Whether it is a one-page press release or a six-page strategy, documents provide a platform, an invitation, for everyone to contribute.

I have found this approach allows the introverted and analytically minded of the group to bring their best thinking forward. It allows those who read and process quickly to review their notes to identify the highest priority feedback before the discussion begins. Reading a common document allows people in a meeting room and those on the phone or video conference to fully participate in the discussion, which is increasingly critical in our distributed work teams. No matter if you are a junior or senior team member, you can contribute. No matter your age, race, religion, location, or native language, you can contribute. In diverse teams, this helps build inclusivity.

Documents are faster: I have participated in highly complex strategy discussions where we handled topics that would have taken hours to present linearly but were consumed fully in a fifteen-to-twenty-minute document read, leaving more time for a rich discussion of the whole idea and its implications. Because everyone on the read can fully participate, this leads to much richer feedback, getting to the heart of the issues faster, and is a better use of everyone's time as no one is tempted to just read your PowerPoint slides. I found writing documents takes more time than creating a bulleted presentation, but practice makes them go faster. And at scale across an organization, faster, better meetings with leadership can have a marked influence on the speed of the whole organization. Amazon is admired for being an innovative company, and I am convinced that the writing culture enabling high velocity decision making is why.

Documents bring clarity: Verbal presentations or open-ended discussions permit informational "Jell-O." There is an adage that "you can't pin Jell-O to the wall," meaning it can't be held in a solid position for long.

Attendees might ask, "Did we decide on exactly what was in the presentation or what was said in the meeting?" Those who did not attend the meeting can find out-of-context PowerPoint slides impossible to decipher, especially ones that follow great design principles like big fonts, few words, and lots of pictures. That type of slide design might work great for a one-directional TED talk or a keynote presentation, but they are very damaging in smaller meetings meant to arrive at decisions.

This lack of clarity leads not only to the potential for *smoke and mirrors* charlatan behavior, but it also can make decisions vague. And vague decisions are hard to implement, so they are inherently doomed from the start.

Since leaving Amazon, I find myself writing documents to support summary PowerPoint presentations ensuring that I am thinking deeply and keeping the customer ever in the forefront. These documents can be a simple one page that describes the purpose, some background or context, the alternatives considered, and the final recommendation. Or they can be more elaborate documents, with reference appendices, that document complex workstreams, and analysis. Writing can document the decision and serve as a reference for stakeholders moving forward.

Ambiguity kills organizations slowly, and clarity speeds things up. When you can get richer and more meaningful feedback on key strategic issues faster, as I have seen with the document process, you can speed up your whole organization to make better decisions faster. And when you have a detailed document of the decision, this has a huge impact across the organization and can lead to breakthroughs for customers and real competitive advantages.

Writing makes you a better leader (and everyone is a leader): Cognitive psychologist Ronald Kellogg explains how thinking and writing are the "twins of mental life." Writing is more challenging because it demands thinking and is a means for thinking. I have observed leaders being apologetic about their writing skills (and some rightfully so). While those who claim they "aren't writers" generally mean that they aren't talented at novels or other works of great art. In doing so, they discount the fact that writing is so closely tied to thinking. Far fewer people would protest, "But I'm not a thinker!"

Leaders must be thinkers but also great communicators. Great leaders have a high degree of emotional intelligence that comes through self-reflection. Writing is the foundation for all three. And because writing and thinking are so closely aligned, writing can make you a better reader of the strategies proposed by others.

WRITING AS PLANNING

Alexandra Carter is the Director of the Columbia Law School Mediation Clinic. She advises her clients to take five minutes to consider and write down the problem they want to solve with a negotiation or a decision they are making before the first conversation occurs.

"Include any issues that you think may have contributed to the situation as it stands today, as well as the effects of these issues are having on your life, career, company, or community," she advises. From that longer piece, she advises her clients to summarize the background, analysis, and emotions into one sentence. "Summarizing your problem in one sentence helps to give you the clearest, most concise picture possible," she said.

Carter advises taking anything negative and backward-looking and reframing it to the positive and forward-looking. A "we need to stop losing money on this line of business" becomes "we need to start making a profit on this line of business by the end of the second quarter."

The final step she recommends is to take that summary sentence and change it into a question beginning with "how, what, who, or when." The sentence would then become "How can we start making a profit on this line of business by June?" or "What would need to change to make this business profitable in two quarters?" Before you write or consider a proposal or approach a big decision, it is useful to think deeply, with pen or keyboard in hand, about what this issue means to you and your business so that you can enter the conversation with clarity of purpose.

Charles Kettering, who was the head of research at General Motors for twenty-seven years, founder of Delco, and holder of 186 patents, said, "a problem well-stated is a problem half-solved." This is true of the business decisions you will face and how you approach those decisions as a leader.

Within a few months of joining Amazon in 2018, I thought I'd take a stab at writing a PR/FAQ to propose a new tool for our business. Reflecting back, I broke every rule. I squeezed it onto one page by thinning the margins and shrinking the font. I didn't talk to customers first. I didn't really clarify who my customer was and what problem I was trying to solve (mine was a very myopic approach). I got a few people who were experts in the space to provide some feedback, but the idea never went anywhere near implementation. I learned that just like the *Velveteen Rabbit*, ideas must be loved into existence. After writing it out and getting some feedback, I was not in love. With diligent work on the document, I understood the problem better and knew that my time was better spent elsewhere. This is the power of written strategy.

Fast forward to 2020 and I was asked to envision a business-wide initiative to crowd-source big ideas to inform our strategic plans. That document came together more easily, gained momentum through the reads, and was received and approved enthusiastically by our entire leadership team. It was subsequently implemented across the business in a number of weeks and delivered results that were four times greater than our projections. The process of writing, which I had practiced extensively since that first PR/FAQ, served the strategy and resulted in better, faster decisions.

Kyle Wiens is the CEO of iFixit, an online repair community. In the process of trying to communicate more clearly, they set a policy that they would not hire people who had sloppy grammar, and they codified their writing in what became the Tech Writing Handbook. Wiens goes as far as to say that "your company is only as good as your writing."

The same can be said of leaders. Writing is the highest form of thinking, combining the unique human capabilities of expression and thought. Now, I don't go as far as to vilify the use of PowerPoint. It has its place. However, the better you are at writing and fostering writing skills in your organization, the better leader you will be—at the time of the decision and long after. And who knows, you might save a life.

PRO TIPS:
- Write out your strategy or your proposed decisions.
- Read and invite others to read and provide feedback.
- Remember brevity is strategy. Clear, concise language represents clearer thinking.
- Become a student of writing. Take a class, read a book, talk to other writers, and most importantly, practice!
- Make writing a key part of your team culture.

CHAPTER 7:

A CASE FOR NOW

"A good plan violently executed now is better than a perfect plan executed next week."

—GENERAL GEORGE S. PATTON

In a very entertaining TED talk, Tim Urban, the cartoonist and author behind the *Wait but Why* website, describes the mind of a procrastinator. It consists of three characters: the *rational decision maker (*who should be at the helm), a *monkey* (the fun-loving distractor of the rational decision maker), and a *panic monster* (who is the only predator of the monkey and who only appears when deadlines approach). He talks about procrastinating writing his college thesis while the monkey in his brain decided to scroll up frame-by-frame the entire length of India on Google Maps "to better get to know the country."

Urban says important, but not urgent, things never trigger the panic monster, so they often do not get prioritized. In people's personal lives, this can be things like putting off meaningful relationships, having children, or travel adventures. In business, these regrets can take the form of risks not taken or opportunities squandered.

At home, procrastination can look like a mindless distraction. However, procrastination dresses up to go to work. Its noble garb can be called *analysis*, *research*, or *discussion*. It can wear the look of busyness when leaders get involved in activities and two-way-door decisions that are not worthy of their attention. They don't delegate and, as a result, cannot attend to the things that *only they* can do. Business leaders who want to appear to all as competent and capable might not admit to being procrastinators. They are much too disciplined and mature for that kind of behavior. Yet, we see that slow decision making impacts businesses dramatically.

A recent McKinsey study found that only 57 percent of public company business leaders surveyed agreed that their organizations consistently made high-quality decisions. Only 48 percent of respondents think that their organizations made decisions quickly. They combined these results and found that faster decision-making processes and faster execution of decisions both correlate to higher returns for the organizations. In fact, organizations that performed best on financial metrics like revenue growth and profit were much more likely to agree that they made fast and high-quality decisions.

"The results indicate that speed and quality outcomes are highly interrelated. According to respondents, the organizations that make decisions quickly are twice as likely to make high-quality decisions, compared with the slow decision-makers," the report concluded.

This was due to three factors they measured: 1) decisions being made at the right level, meaning there was delegation (which ties to the idea we have discussed about talent density),

2) decisions that aligned with corporate strategy and allocated resources to high-value projects (hopefully strategies that address the durable needs of customers), and finally, 3) a commitment to decisions once they were made (which we will talk about in subsequent chapters).

If slowly making decisions has such an impact on business outcomes, why do we do it? As you will see in the following examples, we overestimate the value of being *right*, and we underestimate the drag those slow decisions puts on our organizations. Like a customer returning to a store to buy something they were considering for a while, only to find it sold out, your opportunities might be similarly fleeting. If opportunities are knocking now, they might not wait around outside the door for a long and drawn-out decision-making process, especially, if they are knocking on a two-way door.

SLOW MAKES YOU WRONG

Before you can hope to change the speed of decision making, you must first overcome the myth that slow decisions made with rigor are more likely to be right.

To test your own bias, ask yourself this question:

> *Would you rather be always fast, even if sometimes wrong, or always right, even if sometimes slow?*

Balaji Krishnamurthy, the chairman of ThinkShift, poses this question to the leadership teams he consults. I remember the vigorous debate when he asked the leadership team at Planar this question. If are working on a new bridge that must safely transport millions of vehicles a year over a dangerous river, the right approach is probably slow and right. No one wants to drive on a rushed-to-production bridge.

"When you are instead talking about a new software version for the Apple iWatch, fast and wrong is probably a better choice because it is easily addressed if there is an issue," Krishnamurthy continued. In other words, if it is a one-way door decision, treat it accordingly. If it is a two-way door decision—recognizing that most decisions are—fast is better.

Observing your own team's debate around this question can be a useful assessment of how the organization perceives risk. "If teams have too much of a bias for action, they can introduce risk," Krishnamurthy continued. "If teams are too cautious, they can introduce risk." Managing risk is the role of the leader. And it is easy to forget that there is risk along the time axis of your projects, not just around the return on investment (ROI). If you could make more decisions and only sometimes miss the mark, learning as you go, that will lead to better outcomes than always being right and being late.

Krishnamurthy advises clients that the validity of decisions made today can only be truly understood when time unfolds. If this is true, then speed is of value. If you won't know the results for two years, no matter what data you collect today, then it is better to get on driving toward the point where data will be available and make sure you get there first.

This is important because most companies, including yours and those you compete with, make an alarmingly small set of impactful, one-way door decisions. Marakon Associates, in collaboration with the *Economist* Intelligence Unit, surveyed senior executives from 156 large companies worldwide, each with sales of over one billion dollars, to ask how they thought their planning processes drove strategic decisions. They found that those with strategic planning processes only make 2.5 major strategic decisions a year, the kind that would improve company profits by more than 10 percent in the long term. The authors observed that "it's hard to imagine that with so few strategic decisions driving growth, these companies can keep moving forward and deliver the financial performance the investors expect." Making more decisions can be a competitive differentiator.

SLOW IS EXPENSIVE

Live Nation is a leading live entertainment company bringing over 40,000 shows and more than 100 festivals to life every year, selling 500 million tickets through its brands Ticketmaster, Live Nation Concerts, and Live Nation Sponsorship. They have 44,000 employees globally and sell more concert tickets than anyone else in the world. They are no stranger to risk.

A new president and chief executive officer came in 2005 and committed to lead the transformation of the $10 billion company. This included some big decisions around IT infrastructure. Jake Burns, serving as their vice president of cloud, was a champion of the change and spoke to me recently about his experience.

Over a three-year period, Burns and his team reduced IT costs by 48 percent and improved system availability to more than 99.999 percent (which translates to twenty-six seconds of downtime a month). He was able to do it all without budget impact or a huge bubble of overlapping expenses during the transition. He now advises other CIOs in his role as an enterprise strategist for AWS to set high expectations for performance and speed.

"I think people's expectations are so low that they actually damage their chances of success," he explained. "A leader might come in and say 'we want to transform, and we are going to migrate 50 percent of our applications over three years.' They think that is a big, bold mission, when in fact, that is about a snail's pace. It is so slow that you probably won't be successful if you aim for that."

It is counter-intuitive to believe that companies can fail if they set their goals too low. "It is a phenomenon with large transformations that they are more successful when they happen quickly, and they're less successful when they happen slowly," Burns observed.

He went on to explain. "When you go slowly, you give people a lot of opportunities to think about it, question it, second guess it." But beyond the distraction and speculation, moving slowly can have hard costs. Most people who migrate or implement big system changes have the costs of their current infrastructure, the cost of the infrastructure they are bringing online, and their one-time migration costs. These all hit at once and can cause of bubble of expense. That bubble exists whether your decision is around technology implementation or any other impactful part of your business that involves a transition.

"The longer you drag out the implementation, the larger that bubble is going to be," he continued. "And if the bubble gets too big, then people start saying 'maybe we shouldn't be doing this because it is too expensive.'" This kind of second-guessing can undermine strategy and leadership. Setting goals too low, just to ensure you hit them, can increase costs and jeopardize the whole initiative. This is true not just of technology implementations but of change of all kinds.

PRIORITIZING THE IMPORTANT

Great leaders have to whistle for the panic monster that Tim Urban described. They don't just wait for him to show up.

If you consider the business leaders who have a lasting impact outside of their individual teams, business, or industry, what do they have in common? They created disruption. That disruption is caused not by answering the questions in front of them but by anticipating tomorrow's questions or forcing the answers to questions that no one else is considering. They don't whistle for the monster every week or with every new idea that occurs to them, but they do need to make sure they are creating urgency for strategic change in their business.

If you wait until there is an obvious fork in the road, you are too late, and you have lost the race. Why? Because someone else created the path and set the rules of the game that you now must play.

The truth is, if you are at a strategic fork in the road where the options are clear, you are a follower.

Most forks in the road don't start as high-stakes decisions, thankfully. When done best, they are small experiments, pilots, proofs of concepts, or two-way door decisions, as we have discussed. These small ventures build upon each other in layers of learning until a road is paved.

Followers are faced with high-stakes decisions and a game of catch-up. "Should we abandon our existing legacy business to pursue something that would maintain our competitiveness in the future because we can't afford to do both?" they must ask. To lower the stakes, they are often forced to partner with companies that are further ahead but pose a risk to their business. This working with *frenemies* approach is often the only or best option when it is clear that there is a front-runner, and it isn't you.

How much better would it be to have created the fork in the road and disrupted yourself like Dr. Cook did at Warner Pacific or what played out for Live Nation's cloud architecture. The annuls of business history are littered with companies with dominant positions in their space, with bigger market segment shares, the most loyal customers, and with the best minds in the business, who got left at a turn.

Credited to the general and US President, Dwight Eisenhower, the Urgent-Important Matrix is a classic tool used to sort out prioritization decisions. The two-by-two matrix sorts decisions or projects along two axis to create quadrants based on the relative importance and the relative urgency. Those tasks which are urgent and important, you should do first. The things that are important but not as urgent you should schedule (creating your own deadline to ensure the panic monster arrives on queue). The things that are not as important, but urgent you should delegate. And the things that aren't urgent or important, you should not do. This is a useful tool to force yourself to create your own forks on the road and be ready when circumstances force a decision.

DO THE PREWORK

Gay Gaddis is an author and entrepreneur who judges her decisions along the lines of importance and urgency. She told me in a recent interview that her decision-making process looks to a lot of people to be very abrupt and quick, but that isn't the whole picture.

She founded a firm she called The Think Tank (T3), which sold after 30 years to the LRW Group in 2019. In the years she was running T3, there were times when the business was growing and thriving and other periods where they faced downturns. As a service business, with most of her overhead tied up in personnel salaries, downturns caused staffing decisions to take on new urgency. To stay prepared, she and her management team maintained what she called an "oh shit" list. This was a list of the highest and lowest performers in the company.

"For the top performers, the list reflected the idea that if someone walked out the door, we'd say 'oh, shit' as they'd be hard to replace," Gaddis explained. These were the list of employees so talented and so valuable that were integral to what they were trying to accomplish. "For the bottom performers, the list reflects the idea that if they didn't leave, you might say 'oh shit.'" Demonstrating what Eisenhower called "important, but not urgent," she had her management team keep the list current at all times, not just when they needed to use it.

Maintaining this list allowed them to proactively reward great performers with recognition, promotions, raises, or changing responsibilities that would keep them happy with their job and keep them growing. It allowed her to manage out the talent that wasn't making the grade. It helped maintain their talent density every day. And when tough times forced their hands, they could look at the bottom of the list and see which individuals they had already been talking to about performance.

"This didn't make it easy. Cutting is the worst thing you have to do as a manager, especially if you hired them," Gaddis noted. But because of their regular pattern of data collection and analysis, they could move quickly. "The worst thing you can do in this situation is to dribble people out the door. It makes people nervous and antsy, wondering when the other shoe will drop," she observed. As we have discussed, moving quickly on talent decisions is important, and doing it swiftly builds trust.

She used this same prework approach to the process of selecting a buyer for her business. She had already considered what she wanted, and when the right match came along, she could move quickly, even amidst the uncertainty. She could approach her decision and the eventual implementation with confidence.

MAKING THINGS URGENT (BEFORE IT'S TOO LATE)

According to Danish organizational theorists Kristian Kreiner and Søren Christensen, when we have doubts about a complex choice we are facing, our natural tendency is to defer, even if the consequences are extreme to our businesses, teams, and our reputation as a leader. Their Consequences Model shows how the impact of decisions diminishes over time as your knowledge rises. At some point, those lines cross. On one side of the chart is the land of visionaries and luminaries who are early movers and act without perfect knowledge. On the other side is the land of followers and *also rans* whose knowledge is high, but the market potential is low because others have already gained an advantage.

If you want to disrupt an industry, you can't wait until it is already disrupted. If your competitors are already doing something successfully, thus resulting in more complete knowledge, then it is too late for you to innovate.

"Most leaders over-rotate on being right," Jake Burns continued in our recent discussion. "They are almost exclusively seeking outside perspectives, rather than trying to invent new ways of doing things." And invention is where innovation lives. "Some leaders ask, to the point of annoyance, 'what is everyone else doing?'," he said. "I like to say 'who cares what everyone else is doing.' Instead, let's figure out how you do it."

It is easier said than done, of course. How do you force yourself out of a comfort zone of following to a position of an innovator? This is where the *important but not urgent* box in the Eisenhower Matrix comes into play. Scheduling time and forcing yourself to tackle the important by making it urgent and time-bound is a key to success.

Drs. Daniel Ariely and Klaus Wertenbroch did research on the impact of deadlines on student academic performance. They offered different classes with different deadlines. "We found that the students in the class with the three firm deadlines got the best grades; the class in which I set no deadlines at all (except for the final deadline) had the worst grades; and the class in which they were allowed to choose their own three deadlines (but with penalties for failing to meet them) finished in the middle." Deadlines, even self-imposed ones, led to better performance.

I have seen that same pattern play out in business scenarios in my career. Top-down deadline setting can rally organizations to better-aligned performance. Self-directed goals toward a vision can work nearly as well, but with a lot of variation. And those groups with no pressure to set deadlines might not. There is a reason so much innovation is announced at industry trade shows. They are fixed on the calendar and serve to rally development teams toward a goal.

At his keynote at AWS re:Invent 2019, then AWS CEO Andy Jassy said the secret to digital transformation was senior leadership alignment, conviction, and what he called "top-down aggressive goals." He used GE as an example. "Their CIO, Jamie Miller at the time, decided that they needed to move to the cloud," he said. "She got her top technical leaders together and said, 'We're going to move fifty applications to AWS in thirty days.' And she said for forty-five minutes they told her what a terrible idea this was and how it was impossible. And she said, 'Well, I hear you, but we're going to do it, so let's go.'" In the end, they got to forty-two applications moved in thirty days which her team would have believed impossible. The stretch goal did its job.

Not sure you are moving quickly enough or setting goals high enough? Check the kind of decisions that you are making, and it might be obvious. "Self-evident solutions are evidence of procrastination," Balaji Krishnamurthy offered. If it is obvious to everyone what to do, that is a sure sign that you have waited too long to make the decision. By then, your competitors are already doing it (and gaining the first mover advantage). By then, your customers rising expectations makes your previously strong offering weaker every day. If you find yourself playing catch-up, it might not just be your industry or bad luck. It could be a bad process or a call to leadership.

TOMORROW IS NOT GUARANTEED

Becki Saltzman, an expert on decision-making processes, told me recently, "Time has its fingers on the scale of long-term outcomes." Because you don't know the results of a decision until much later, staying power is critical. Sadly, many businesses don't have time. Every day companies go bankrupt and close. It is estimated that 90 percent of new start-ups fail, with just over 50 percent of businesses making it to the fifth year and only 25 percent of businesses making it to the fifteen-year mark. Eighty-two percent of businesses fail because of cash flow problems.

Joel Bines, managing director of the consulting firm AlixPartners' retail practice, summed up the relationship well when he told *RetailDive*, "Money equals time, and time equals options. It's a very simple equation. The more money you have, the more time you have; the more time you have, the more options you have. That's like E=mc2 for turnarounds." Those who don't survive can never focus on the important, because the urgent overtakes them. Time eventually catches up.

During the NCAA college basketball tournament in 2021, AT&T ran a funny series of advertisements explaining the rules of sports. In a spot called "Lily Uncomplicates: Buzzer Beaters," the actress sits at an anchor desk in an AT&T store and offers this advice: "To beat the buzzer, just shoot earlier." Although it is exciting to see a last-ditch effort lead to an unexpected win in an athletic game, that is not how you want to run your business or your team. "It all comes down to punctuality, folks," the commercial continues. If you manage the pace of your own game, you can set yourself up to win today and into the future.

PRO TIPS:
- Evaluate what kind of decisions you are making. If they are self-evident, resolve to make more decisions faster.
- Whistle for the panic monster. Make decisions before you are forced to. Set deadlines.
- Do the prework to decide what is important to you.
- Remember, slow is expensive and can lead an organization to splintering self-doubt. Move quickly toward ambitious goals.
- Avoid a buzzer beater.

CHAPTER 8:

PLACING YOUR BET

"Personal decisions are the leading cause of death."

—DR. RALPH KEENEY, AUTHOR ON THE TOPIC
OF DECISION ANALYSIS AND VALUE-FOCUSED
THINKING, PROFESSOR EMERITUS AT DUKE AND
THE UNIVERSITY OF SOUTHERN CALIFORNIA

If you have ever been nervous making a decision, then congratulations. You are alive, and you care!

At this point in the book, we have covered a lot of ground. We have talked about how talent, a focus on customers and process, and speed all contribute to well-made decisions. Now is where we get personal.

The myth of the inspired, solitary decision maker making good and bad decisions is perpetuated by the fact that the stakes of decisions can be high, and we naturally want someone to blame or credit for the outcomes. Journalists love to report about how a leader destroyed enterprise value or grew their company. They look for someone to blame or credit for derailing an iconic brand or building it to new prominence. They constantly look to discover and highlight who was responsible for what was deemed a brilliant or horrific acquisition. The ultimate perceived success or failure will propel or constrain a leader's next steps and bolster or soil their reputation. For this reason, any high-stakes business decision is seen as a career decision and thus is highly personal.

BETTING ON YOURSELF

"To make decisions, especially big ones like deciding to sell your company, dissolve a partnership, or bring on new partners, you must have the confidence to believe that you can make the outcome what you want it to be," described Josh Stump in a recent interview where he described his work as an attorney and president of Buckley Law advising clients with some of the biggest decisions of their lives. Likening it to driving a car, he added, "The initial big turn is a lot less important in your mind if you know you can get to your destination by going left or right." He admitted, "It might be hubris, but the good leaders I see making decisions aren't necessarily betting on the decision. They are betting on themselves."

"I like the phrase 'sometimes in error, but never in doubt,'" he continued. This doesn't mean one should make decisions arbitrarily. After all, that is why his clients seek out expert counsel in the first place. "But when I see people who are repetitively successful," he added, "I see people who are confident in their ability to keep making decisions after the big one."

This idea of betting on yourself might feel like overconfidence. Blake Shelton, a staple on the reality television show *The Voice*, once justified an exaggerated sales pitch he made to a contestant by saying, "I might be full of crap, but I am never deterred." It got a laugh (and the contestant may have chosen him as their coach if I recall correctly). If we are honest, we see the same tenacity in leaders. The smart ones know that they might make mistakes, but they are confident enough to persist and course correct along the way, hopefully with the input of others.

In her best-selling book, the *Growth Mindset*, and related TED talk, Stanford University psychologist Dr. Carol Dweck identified that people who believe they can learn and change, perform better in every arena of their lives. They measure themselves not on whether they pass or fail at any point in time but will give themselves a rating of "not yet" as they continue toward mastery. They believe that a bet on themselves will pay off given enough time and energy.

Any decision of consequence (like writing a book, as a case in point) could be called an act of overconfidence. When I sit down to write, I have no idea how readers will receive the work (but like Blake Shelton, I am undeterred). The same is true of other decisions I regularly make when the outcome is unknown. You have to believe you will overcome any obstacles that lie ahead.

It is a pattern I have seen time after time in successful leaders in different situations. Chip Gaines helped secure a pilot for the HGTV hit show *Fixer Upper* in what some would call an act of idiocy: he bought a boat on which he thought his growing family would live, sight unseen, and surprised his unsuspecting wife. When that and other bets turned out okay, they bought some run-down property in their hometown of Waco, Texas, which became the Magnolia Silos retail location. It was a very large investment that amounted to putting it on all the line. "We had no idea what the future held for the show. It could be over tomorrow," he said. "With the future uncertain, the thought of sinking everything into such a large property was completely terrifying."

Crediting his faith for his resilience, he summarized risk taking in this way: "For people with a winner mentality, there's a positive waiting for you no matter the outcome." In contrast, for those with a pessimistic outlook, every setback brings a sense of failure. "That's why I always say winning and losing isn't an event. It's a mindset," Gaines concluded. Outlasting requires confidence.

Elon Musk, CEO and founder of Tesla Motors, has regularly made headlines with his bold moves. When the company promised delivery of the Model 3, which was dogged with delays on the production line in 2017, he admitted "we were a little overconfident" and that they "got too comfortable with our ability to do battery modules." He went on to reference his other company's, SpaceX, Falcon Heavy's maiden voyage earlier that year and quipped, "If we can send a Roadster to the asteroid belt, we can probably solve Model 3 production." Their earlier missteps had a negative impact, but he remained undeterred. Now the Tesla Model 3 is the world's best-selling plug-in electric vehicle (EV).

Customers would not have confidence in the cars had Tesla's leadership not acknowledged and fixed the issues caused by their over-confidence. There would be no Tesla if leadership hadn't been "over-confident." It is about striking a balance. Great leaders are not blinded by their confidence but recognize the role it plays in their success.

Not surprisingly, self-confidence is linked to a happy and fulfilling life, according to Dr. Barbara Markway, author of *The Self-Confidence Workbook*. These include less fear and anxiety, greater motivation, more resilience, improved relationships, and a stronger sense of where your purpose and principles lie. And these are all factors that lead to better outcomes from business decisions, as well, if you have the confidence to admit being wrong, to avoid procrastination, to delegate, and to rally people toward the future.

Interestingly, scientific research is beginning to understand that although confidence has roots in personality, it is a learned trait. Dr. Amy Cuddy's famous TED talk spoke about how the simple act of standing "like a superhero" for a few minutes before an act of bravery can improve confidence and risk tolerance. If a few minutes of power posing can change our mindset and that our mindset can change our outcomes, imagine what years of making business decisions and observing the results can do! Confidence, or lack thereof, is an emotion that comes easily to some but can be developed in others. Having the right emotions can put you in a mindset to win long-term.

FEELINGS ARE DATA

"The truth is that a tremendous amount of business decisions are emotional," Josh Stump continued. "We make an assumption that once you reach a level of sophistication or business acumen, you are awarded with Vulcan thinking and are purely logical." Once promoted to leadership, are the decisions of those individuals based only on research and reason? Hardly. Yet, there is an assumption that if a decision ends up being wrong or fails to achieve its potential, it is because you didn't have the right data.

"The reality is even sophisticated business leaders who hold titles like chief executive officer, general counsel, and chief legal officer, do not make decisions in this way," Stump added. Their emotions play a huge role in decision making, and their confidence makes all the difference in the outcomes.

If confidence will contribute motivation, resilience, the ability to work with people, and stay true to your purpose, then it is critical, not just in making the decision but throughout implementation. "The aftermath of decision making is less fixed and known than people might think," Stump continued. "It might be a decision you can't unwind, but even in those cases, there is still a big spectrum of things that can transpire in the future." He referenced a client lawsuit that was in negotiation. The client "might settle the case, but there are a lot of things still on the table," he concluded. "Choices, even big ones, don't lock you into a single choice from there on out." And knowing that should make us all a bit more confident.

IT ALL ADDS UP

As we have explored, in most contexts, especially in high-stakes business environments, decisions are not singular events but rather fit into a portfolio and a life cycle. They have a context rooted in culture and mindset. They have a history, and they have a future. And those decisions add up and compound, just like interest on principle in an investment, to create (or diminish) value.

Dr. Ralph Keeney has written and lectured extensively on decision analysis. When speaking about how value-based decision making shows up in our personal lives, he made a bold claim that the leading cause of death in America isn't cancer or heart disease, nor is it smoking or obesity. And it isn't PowerPoint. "It's our inability to make smart choices and overcome our own self-destructive behaviors," he said. Most of us don't decide to weaken our hearts, clog our arteries, or expose ourselves to fatal risks in a single decision. It is the cumulative effect of a lifetime of choices, like sitting at a desk instead of standing. It's poor eating choices repeated throughout a lifetime. The same can occur in our businesses.

It's a diet of decisions that make our companies.

The talent density of your organization and the ways of making decisions that we had examined in this book thus far are not the result of a single decision maker acting alone. You make hiring decisions. Those employees, in turn, implement new processes, write new strategies, and uncover new customer insights—thousands and hundreds of thousands of decisions layering to create the outcomes.

Even seemingly independent decisions are more inter-related than you might think. All because we are creatures of habit and because of our innate biases. Here are just a few that illustrate the point.

Past successes make us blind to the risk of loss. Behavioral economist Dr. Richard Thaler talked about how a logical bias contributed to the stock market bubble in the early 2000s and the housing crisis a few years later. "Part of the reasoning seemed to be that they had made so much money in recent years that even if the market fell, they would only lose those newer gains," he said. Of course, when the market turned, people saw real losses, and those "investors who were highly leveraged lost much more than house money. Many also lost their homes." So leaders would do well to avoid the overconfidence that can come from a short view of history.

Poor business performance can make us impulsive. Thaler's research revealed that "mutual fund portfolio managers take more risks in the last quarter of the year when the fund they are managing is trailing the benchmark index to which their returns are compared." In an effort to break even, gambling when behind is rarely a winning strategy on the tables of Las Vegas or Monaco, and certainly not in portfolio management. He advised leaders to pay attention to the behavior of employees who were losing money. And if you are the one losing money, you need to make sure you're seeking and getting wise counsel.

Performance management can make us timid. His further research indicates that "a manager is loss averse regarding any outcomes that will be attributed to him." In other words, if you are publicly accountable for the results, you will act more conservatively. Even if, as we discussed, those behaviors lead to worse outcomes. This can be driven by a sense of personal responsibilities or by corporate reward and punishment structures. "In many companies, creating a large gain will lead to modest rewards, while creating an equal-sized loss will get you fired," Thaler observed. Make commitments thoughtfully, and do not let them unduly influence your risk tolerance.

Bias can make good people discriminate. We may have implicit biases against issues and people that result in uncharitable and inequitable actions. No matter our intentions, we have biases. We are capable of raising our awareness and our skills in interrupting those bias to do better work. As psychologist Dr. Dolly Chung writes, "Becoming the person we mean to be starts with a look at ourselves." Beware of judging yourself by your intentions and others by their behaviors or appearances.

KNOWING WHAT YOU WANT

I had enrolled in an executive MBA program at Pepperdine University and was excited to get started. I had chosen a program that was not local which required me to take a short flight to the Bay Area in California every three weeks for

Friday and Saturday workshops. I was paying for the program myself, including the flights, and had asked for some flexibility in my hours to accommodate the lectures and study. I had selected a thesis related to our business with input from our CEO (aimed to uncover how we might move into a faster-growing market). I felt some schedule flexibility was a small ask for a salaried employee investing above-and-beyond in the company, so the reaction to my proposed schedule change puzzled and infuriated me. I had not been thanked for my willingness to invest in the business, but instead had been asked to take a pay cut. This was untenable, so I asked for a meeting with the head of human resources and organizational development. She listened to me rant and then asked me a very important question: "Jennifer, what is it that you want?"

It was more than the money, of course. I wanted the recognition that the investment I was putting into my skill set would be appreciated and rewarded. Not just today, but in the future for which I was busily preparing. It was clear this was not going to happen at my current employer, and it saddened me. Within a few short months, I left the company, taking a new opportunity at a company that supported my education and at which I saw a career path and a chance to learn new things. It was a very difficult decision—harder, perhaps, than it should have been. I was disappointed that I wasn't being seen. I was angry about the sacrifices I was being asked to make and was confused as to why it had come to this. However, I had not been clear in my mind what I wanted to happen next. Her question set me off on a different and better path.

Apparently, I am not alone. "In my mediation work, I find one of the most common sources of disputes is people not seeing and presenting themselves as you are," said Alexandra

Carter, a mediator and professor who wrote the book, *Ask for More*. "Honestly ask—what do I need? It helps you get to the root of any problem or negotiation. And it takes practice and patience to answer it fully."

When asked about his purchase of the *Washington Post*, Jeff Bezos reflected that "If you can make a decision with analysis, you should do so. But it turns out in life that your most important decisions are always made with instinct and intuition, taste, heart." If the newspaper "had been a financially upside-down salty snack food company, I would not have bought it." In contrast, in the newspaper investment, he saw a larger legacy in democracy. He knew what he wanted, and that clarity informed the decision.

Drs. Chip and Dan Heath are professors at Stanford and Duke, respectively, who have studied decision making extensively. They contend clarifying questions they recommend asking—like "What kind of organization do you aspire to run?" or "What's best for your team in the long run?"—are not questions with one right answer. "Those are emotional questions—speaking to the passions and value and beliefs—and when you answer them, there's no 'rational machine' underneath that is generating your perspective," they said. "It's just who you are and what you want. The buck stops with emotion."

As was the case with my decision to change jobs in graduate school, emotions might help inform the decision you make. "Be aware of the emotions that come up as you proceed with your decision," said Larina Kase, the author of *The Confident Leader*. "Accept the emotions and allow them to guide you without controlling you." Your feelings are data points you can use to make and implement better decisions. Note them, get curious, and learn from them.

IT'S YOUR STORY

Learning from past decisions in order to make new ones is illustrated well in a movie starring Shirley McLaine and Amanda Seyfried entitled *The Last Word*. McLaine plays a cranky octogenarian who strives to improve how her ambitious and accomplished legacy will be remembered. She hires the newspaper's obituary writer, studies the four factors that make up a great obituary, and sets about to change her life. Well, at least to change her final story to something more flattering.

In a poignant scene in the movie, McLaine's character declares: "You don't make mistakes. Mistakes make you smarter. They make you stronger, and they make you more self-reliant." The difference is the mindset.

If you have experienced setbacks and mistakes, you have an advantage over those who never endured and had to dig deep to survive. If you notice a pattern of struggle or failure, you can know you're on your way from a *not yet* into mastery. The difference isn't the failure or setback. It is what you did with it. If you're feeling a lot of emotion around a decision, look at it objectively and get curious.

Sara Blakely, the founder of Spanx, spoke to this concept in a Tweet using a phrase only a shapewear company CEO could. Borrowing the words of Gary Lew, she posted: "This is your world. Shape it or someone else will." She added, "Don't let anyone else wear your life. It's yours and yours alone to shape."

Lives and careers, like decisions, need to be crafted and made. Make a good one.

PRO TIPS:

- Treat your feelings as data points. Get curious about your emotions to better understand the real issues behind the decision.
- Know what you want.
- Remain self-aware of your tendencies, temptations, and biases.
- Study your decision making for patterns and results.
- Change your story if you don't like it.

CHAPTER 9:

DISCOVERING CULTURE

———

"Determine what behaviors and beliefs you value as a company, and have everyone live true to them. These behaviors and beliefs should be so essential to your core, that you don't even think of it as culture."

—BRITTANY FORSYTH, SENIOR VICE PRESIDENT
OF HUMAN RESOURCES, SHOPIFY

"Why is culture so important to a business?" asked Brian Chesky, cofounder and CEO of Airbnb, in an internal employee memo in 2013. "The stronger the culture, the less corporate process a company needs."

It is like going to the symphony as compared to going to a stadium concert. You don't have to post a dress code on the door of the concert hall or tell people to speak more quietly as they find their assigned velvet-upholstered seats. They take their cues from others, dress up, and act differently than they would at a stadium rock concert. That is the power of culture.

"When the culture is strong, you can trust everyone to

do the right thing," Chesky added. Airbnb has been able to do that at scale: from its humble start twelve years ago when they posted some air mattresses in the founder's own apartment (inspiring the name) to their initial public offering in December of 2020 with a valuation of $47 billion.

You could have detailed policy manuals turning every possible scenario into instructions, but that is not practical in a fast-moving business or those with highly skilled or highly trained talent. This is where culture is crucial: "when the boss isn't in the room, when there are no rules or processes written for a said situation," explained Daniel Weinand, who served as the chief culture officer at Shopify.

Culture matches the talent density we discussed earlier, with the needs of customers. When reinforced by mechanisms, like writing, it produces better outcomes from every decision that is made.

DISCOVERING CULTURE

The late Tony Hsieh was a serial entrepreneur who helped found the online shoe retailer Zappos, which was acquired by Amazon in 2009 for $1.2 billion in stock. He believed corporate culture could help promote happiness. This echoes research by Glassdoor about the link between employee well-being and customer satisfaction, with the highest correlation in roles with the highest customer contact.

Facing a scaling problem as the business grew, he and other senior leaders couldn't possibly interview everyone they hired. They wanted to maintain talent density and preserve the culture. As Hsieh put it, only a handful of leaders had gotten good at finding employees that were "a little weird, not psycho snake weird." With criteria like that, no wonder why they had difficulty scaling hiring in those days!

It was suggested that Hsieh come up with a list of core values to serve as a guide for managers to make hiring decisions. He grabbed a pen and jotted down ideas, which, as we discussed, is a great way to clarify strategy. "I thought about all the employees I wanted to clone because they represented the Zappos culture well and tried to figure out what values they personified," he explained.

Similarly, he thought about all the employees or ex-employees who were not culture fits, and he "tried to figure out where there was a value disconnect." This became his own version of Gay Gaddis' "oh shit list.". He made a list of thirty-seven potential core values and shared them out across the company and, over the course of a year, got feedback and suggestions, publishing their first values document on February 14: a kind of Valentine's Day love note to the company. At the top of the list was the idea of wowing their customers.

Based on these values, Zappos became famous for outlandishly good and quirky customer service. As an illustration, Hsieh sent an email to a customer whose shipment had been delayed. Alongside his apology was an invitation to call and "Ask whoever answers the phone to do something weird or embarrassing, like sing 'I'm a Little Teacup' or do their best audio impression of a cute kitten. If there is anything we can do to get a little smile out of you, just let us know what it is and we'll do our best to accommodate." Only those who were a little weird but not psycho-snake weird would be able to care for customers in this way.

Once onboard, new employees receive an offer of $3,000 to leave the company. Even if they are doing well, the belief is that after training and working with customers in the call center, if one hadn't committed to the goals and culture, Zappos would prefer them to leave. The approach is working.

They report repeat sales from their current customers to account for more than 75 percent of revenue.

Hsieh's experience echoes the advice of Jeff Bezos in his 2018 Amazon shareholder letter: "You can write down your corporate culture, but when you do so, you're discovering it, uncovering it—not creating it." And after you discover it, you must nurture it.

CALIBRATING CULTURE

When Howard Schultz rejoined Starbucks as CEO in 2008, one of the first moves was implementing what they called an "Espresso Excellence Training." This event shut down the stores to customers for three hours of in-depth upskilling in the art of espresso. This move cost the company six million dollars and spawned negative press as critics claimed the company was broken beyond repair. After an era of brand extensions into food and music, this decision sent a powerful message to their employees and customers that Starbucks was serious about coffee.

"People go out of calibration just like machines go out of calibration," said CEO Thomas Crosby from Pal's Sudden Service, a regional fast-food chain that is the only restaurant to win the coveted Malcolm Baldridge Quality Award. "So we are always training, always teaching, always coaching. If you want people to succeed, you have to be willing to teach them. Even in a business with lots of lower-skilled employees, investing in culture is an effort in constant calibration and shows big rewards." In fact, companies with many entry-level employees may find their training systems are primarily responsible for maintaining their talent density.

When Schultz returned to lead Starbucks, he found that the smell of burnt cheese from their new food offerings—not the smell of fine coffee—greeted guests at the door. The company culture had gone out of calibration, and everyone could smell it.

Schultz demonstrated what leaders at all levels should recognize: they are the Chief Cultural Officer of their organizations. It isn't just about what is said in speeches or plastered on posters that define and reinforces the culture. Commitment to culture is reflected in training we discussed at Starbucks and Pal's Sudden Service and policies like those at Zappos who would rather pay people to leave if they weren't committed to *wow* customers. These are acts of culture.

CULTURE AS A MIRROR OF LEADERSHIP

After several years at a privately-held educational software start-up, I joined Planar, a public company that had thousands of employees around the world. It was led by its founder CEO, Jim Hurd. Hurd was in no small way our chief cultural officer. He lived the values reflected in his company.

Believing Helsinki hotels to be far too expensive, he slept in the Finland factory when he visited. He apparently would shower in the sauna area (yes, the factory had a sauna. It was Finland, after all). Years later, when I visited, the sauna was mainly used for storage, but an employee giving me a tour could point out the couch on which Hurd had slept. I tried to imagine his tall and lanky frame laying on this small couch and him smoothing his shock of strawberry blonde hair each morning using the little mirror on the wall. Perhaps it is no surprise that the company he founded was also frugal with unadorned offices and conservative investments. Employees in the Finland factory probably didn't need detailed policies to keep their spending in check. They had the CEO sleeping in the sauna to remind them.

Hurd and his cofounders were innovators. At Planar's founding in 1983, they dreamed of full-color electronic displays that would be so thin and light that they could hang on the wall, roll up for portability, and be put into miniaturized computers. The company archives still include the first laptop (which could actually fit on a lap) with a Planar flat-panel display. During my time there, we continued to innovate with award-winning, differentiated products. Innovation was in the DNA. It was something you could trace back to the company's founding fathers that showed up in product design and also in the offices themselves.

Planar had spun out of the research and development labs of a test and measurement company. All the founders were scientists accustomed to working in open lab spaces. The executive suite (singular) was a bullpen, with a smattering of desks and an all-glass conference room in the corner (appropriately called the "fishbowl"). Everyone could hear everyone's conversations and couldn't help but work as a team. Transparency ruled the day.

The home-spun values rooted in manufacturing—things like frugality, collaboration, and innovation—fueled the company for many years and drove the strategy. Every year the highest honor awarded was the Yoda award, named after the famous green Jedi master of Star Wars fame. On it was written, "There is no try, there is only do." That pretty much summed up the company. We didn't really talk much about the values. We just did them as the guide on the side of our customers.

When I went to work for Intel, it was my first experience with a highly purposeful and articulated corporate culture. It started for me with my first day at "New Employee Integration." Everyone who was new that week shuffled into a conference room where we heard executive presentations about the company values. They were on plaques up around the campus and mentioned in all-hands presentations and investor materials. Like all values that are real, they served as the foundation for the hiring and employee evaluations.

After several interesting assignments at Intel, I was recruited back to Planar to join an internal start-up selling flat-panel desktop monitors. From that vantage point of this new business down the street from the Planar headquarters, it was easy to observe the changes from the earlier era.

The new Planar CEO, Balaji Krishnamurthy, who we met earlier in the book, is also an energetic leader and a scientist, but there the similarities with Hurd end. Under his leadership, the executive bullpen became a series of offices because he wanted space to think, pace, and process his ideas out loud without disrupting others. The informal culture rooted in manufacturing innovation was replaced by an intentional culture with large ambitions to put a display in front of every human and build a brand.

For the lobby of a new building, Krishnamurthy commissioned a towering painting of horses running in bold, abstract colors. This is how he saw the company. Ambitious, colorful, and tied to history (after all, the first displays were cave paintings drawn by hunting parties). The sweeping strokes and rush of the horses implied the boldness that was part of the new value set and what he wanted employees to feel viscerally when they entered the building.

That is what culture does. It helps employees feel their way. It helps them know how to make and implement decisions aligned with leadership.

CHANGING CULTURE

Harkening back to our reflections on talent density, you can change the culture—and by extension, the ability of the organization to make and implement decisions—by changing the composition of the staff, but only so fast. This is why so many organizations start "intrapreneurial" or entrepreneurial-spirited tiger teams outside the core of the business. There they can develop new products or open new markets, but also create a new culture so those businesses can succeed. This is what my time at Intel and my early days back at Planar represented. At Intel, the setup of new business groups, like mine in online computing, was an intentional effort not to let the culture squash change.

Craig Barrett, who was CEO at Intel when I worked there, likened the company's core microprocessor business to a creosote bush, the desert plant that poisons the ground under and around it so that no new seeds can sprout. Barrett feared that the semiconductor business would kill other innovations within Intel. This poison can take several forms. Perhaps cash would not be available for new initiatives because it was tied up in past property, plant, and equipment investments. Perhaps there were unrealistic margin expectations or a skill-set misalignment. Great businesses are poisoned before they can take root. Sometimes this looks like a full organ rejection of a transplant, with the new business and its leaders fighting internal politics and policies at every turn. In other cases, I have seen new start-up businesses poisoned by good intentions, visibility, oversight, and too much pressure to achieve profit too soon.

This is very true when companies embark on large-scale digital transformation. Questions like "Should we have an app?" or "Could we offer a subscription for recurring revenue?" may start to change the offerings of these companies, but perhaps not at the level required for sustainable success or true differentiation in the market. Boston Consulting Group (BCG) did a study and found that "digital transformation requires instilling a culture that supports the change while enabling the company's overarching strategy." Having the will isn't enough. There has to be a way.

Decisions at this level of impact require leadership to acknowledge that a change is necessary and to be able to articulate what good looks like. Not just what good technology implementations or good financial results look like, but the day-to-day behaviors of the company that will lead to those outcomes. This is critical because culture provides a framework for decision making at all levels of the organization. Like the painting in the Planar lobby, sometimes you have to see it to feel it, and you have to feel it to get it.

DISRUPT YOURSELF TO DISRUPT YOUR CULTURE

Cultures, even ones that are unarticulated, are reinforced with a mix of possibility and fear. This is what Gerry Perkel, then CEO of Planar, noticed was going on during a discussion about product strategy several years ago.

As I have shared, the business had acquired a very successful video wall company, Clarity Visual Systems. Planar was considering its next moves in important markets like control rooms (where video walls were used to display decision-making data) or digital signage advertising. "At the time, our main products in this category were highly profitable 'rear-projection cubes,' as we called them," Perkel explained in a recent interview. These cubes would stack together like Lego bricks with virtually no space between them to create seamless walls of video. There was a new liquid crystal display (LCD) technology coming that promised to create thinner walls but with more space between the displays. The question on the table in the board room that day was whether or not Planar should develop a product using the new technology. But like many decisions, more was at stake than that.

"We knew it might obsolete products in which we enjoyed a sizable market share and customer loyalty," Perkel recalled. This new effort would divert talent and budget away from established product lines. It would put Planar in head-to-head competition with some new players in the market, who had established themselves as consumer electronic or appliance brands. As a publicly traded company, it was also important to meet current and future profit expectations. The undercurrent of the concern was that a move to LCD could change the way customers perceived the brand and the value that employees felt they were bringing to the customers. It was a question of identity, as much as technology.

As he listened to the debate, Perkel leaned his six-foot-four-inch frame back in his seat, and his mind drifted to a story someone had told him years before. A friend of his was working for Kodak and devised a strategy for the digital camera market when few were in the space, and the leaders had not yet been established. Perkel's friend presented his proposal eagerly to a group of experienced Kodak executives. One of them, an older, well-respected company veteran, spoke for the group saying, "Young man, we are in the chemical business. We make an 80 percent gross margin. Why would I want to be in a 30 percent gross margin business?" The discussion ended. Kodak stayed out of digital imaging for decades. Business schools now study this as an epic failure.

A visit to Kodak's office in Rochester, New York, in 2004 gave me a strong sense of the culture. I drove to the campus in frigid winter weather and passed through large concrete fences with barbed wire on top. The complex was about as welcoming as a Siberian prison. After parking the car, I was directed to a small outbuilding that smelled of dust and metal. I picked up a phone that rang the front desk, where I introduced myself to someone who reluctantly buzzed me in from the cold into an austere lobby. The inhospitable coldness of the day mirrored how I felt as a visitor.

It was clear they were protecting something, not welcoming in anything new. Their success had become their creosote bush, and they put up walls. It was clear they were fearful and isolated from the world outside upstate New York. It was no surprise to me that Kodak didn't recognize the real threat or the opportunity that lay ahead of them in digital cameras years ago.

"Kodak was heading into the unknown but didn't know it," Perkel thought. "It is too easy a temptation for those who enjoy superiority of brand or cost in their current category."

The conversation in the Planar conference room had shifted from margin to product performance and specifications. For years, the team had worked to drive down the bezel width between displays to a fraction of what they would be in these LCD video walls. Customer feedback and research were consistent that seamless was preferred. "Why would anyone want to go back to thicker bezels, even at a lower cost?" someone in the room asked.

Perkel thought about his time at Tektronix, later Xerox, when he ran the color printer division. Laser printers outperformed inkjet printers on virtually any measure. Inkjets were not viewed as serious business equipment but were seen as toys by the incumbents. And yet, they took market share: year after year. They now dominate the space. He reflected on that experience and concluded, "Companies with lower-cost approaches trying to find higher performance almost always beat those with higher-performance trying to chase lower cost." This isn't just a matter of strategy or infrastructure, but one of culture. "What we have always done," can get in the way. It can be a creosote bush to innovation. It can keep leaders from whistling for the panic monster, using Tim Urban's description we discussed earlier, to get the organization to embrace change imperatives.

The conversion continued as the executive and product teams weighed the pros and cons. Perkel then stepped in to offer a perspective, "We are not the only people in the world who can build this product," he said. "Others are coming. They will offer lower-cost products with lower performance to start. But they will get better. The question is not *will* this technology have an impact on our existing offering, but rather *who* will do the disruption. Will we potentially obsolete ourselves or wait for someone else to do it?"

He expressed confidence that the team could find ways to differentiate the offering and leverage the extensive experience with video wall customers. This was a sustaining part of the corporate culture: the innovation and resourceful DNA established years ago to solve customer problems.

Perkel said the conversation changed from asking "if" they were going to do it, to "how" they were going to do it, and excitement grew. The new product was the Planar® Clarity® Matrix LCD video wall which was introduced with fanfare at an industry trade show in 2009.

"The decision to enter that product category didn't make it successful," Perkel recalled. "We had to have great marketing plans. We had to provide exceptional sales training. The strategy wasn't enough. We needed to deliver a good product.

We made it work." This is a common theme when reflecting on great decisions: they prompt other decisions, and those actions lead to results.

"When I think about our approach, versus others in the industry who took a more conservative pace, our brand benefited from us being first to adopt the innovations," Perkel reflected. Being early to market resulted in early customer learnings on which the team could capitalize to which no other competitor had access. We had the benefit of hindsight before anyone else.

For example, soon after the launch, a customer wanted to put a video wall in the corridor of a government building and contacted us, saying the mounting depth was just outside the parameters of the Americans with Disabilities Act (ADA). Although ours was the thinnest on the market, it was still thick enough to cause safety issues for the visually impaired.

In keeping with our culture and aligned to our strategy, we took the customer need to the engineering team. Our talented mechanical designers rose to the challenge and reduced the depth. We now not only had the thinnest, but we had the first and only ADA-compliant video wall on the market. This innovation put Planar ahead of the competition with important federal, state, and local government and institutional customers for years to come. It would not have occurred if the culture hadn't supported innovation. It might not have happened at all if we hadn't gotten the head start with quick decision making.

"There is no such thing as a decision," Perkel concluded. "Each decision delivers a tree of other decisions. Each decision is a step in a journey."

PRO TIPS:

- Discover your culture through thoughtful reflection about how people are successful or fail at your company or within your team.
- Consider how calibrated your employees are to the culture you want to cultivate. Do something about it.
- Look for ways to demonstrate the culture in artifacts, behaviors, and approaches.
- Don't be afraid to disrupt yourself to live your values.

CHAPTER 10:

TREATING TRUTH
AS A GIFT

"Maintaining a firm grasp of the obvious is more difficult than one would think it should be. But it is useful to try."

—JEFF BEZOS, FOUNDER OF AMAZON

"How do you avoid running a company into the ground?"

I was sitting next to our new CEO on a flight and mustered the courage to ask him something that had been on my mind.

"Sometimes new leaders join existing companies and 'run them into the ground'," I said. "This is not your first time stepping into a company. How do you make an existing business better?"

He paused for a moment, perhaps amused by my question as we were taking off. His answer was simple but memorable. "You listen," he said. He went on to tell me that leaders who do poorly stop listening or have people around them that won't tell them the truth (probably because they stopped listening years ago). Your only path to success is to be told the truth. Andy Grove, the famed leader and former CEO of Intel, once quipped: "The CEO is always the last to know." That is even more true if leaders, at any level, don't actively solicit knowledge and if they are not intellectually honest with themselves about what they are hearing.

Confirmation Bias, the inability for us to hear or see things contrary to our held opinions, is a very strong tendency in all of us and has its own gravitational pull. Drs. Chip and Dan Heath, in their book *Decisive* summed it up well: "If we feel a whisker's worth of preference for one option over another, we can be trusted to train our spotlight on favorable data" that will convince us that our preference is correct, and furthermore "supported by thorough analysis."

Just like other personality traits can find themselves mirrored in culture, biases and blind spots of leaders become the bias and blind spots of their teams and organizations.

We all have things we want to hear. The key to great leadership is getting people to tell us anything else. We tend to value what we think more than we should. Sometimes that translates into literal value.

Mathew Hayward and Donald Hambrick then with Columbia University researched 106 large acquisitions and identified factors that contributed to premiums paid. They found that for every favorable article written in a major publication about the acquiring CEO, the acquisition premium rose by 4.8 percent. That means if there are three articles featuring the acquiring CEO, the company would overpay by nearly $29 million on a $200 million acquisition. Note that I said the *acquiring* company. This is the company writing the check. The business they are buying didn't increase in value because of positive publicity. The company *making* the acquisition paid more because *they themselves* had received media coverage.

As someone who sought out favorable coverage for our leaders and products, I can attest leaders should not internalize their press coverage. I have heard of Hollywood actors not reading reviews because if they believe the great ones are true, they have to believe the awful ones have merit as well. The same holds true of business leaders. It feels good to get positive press, but it doesn't make you a better leader or better at making decisions, as that acquisition study demonstrates. Plus, any published news should be talking about things in the past that can be proven and verified, which is not the direction where leaders should be facing—toward the future.

So, what is the anecdote to believing your own press? Hayward and Hambrick found that companies paid lower acquisition premiums when the CEOs had people around them who were more likely to challenge their thinking, such as an independent chairman or board members who were unconnected to the CEO or the company. CEOs need people willing to ask tough questions and tell the truth.

Years after Quaker acquired and then divested Snapple, CEO William Smithburg reflected that "there was so much excitement about bringing in a new brand, a brand with legs. We should have had a couple of people arguing the 'no' side of the evaluation." Are we to believe that Quaker paid $1.7 billion (yes, billion) for Snapple in 1993 and not a single person argued against it? Perhaps the leadership team was blinded by their previous success with the acquisition of Gatorade and thought they could make lightning strike twice without an honest assessment. Perhaps then it is no surprise that Quaker sold Snapple just four years later to Triarc for a mere seventeen cents on the dollar. Somewhere along the way, people had stopped telling the truth and it cost the company $1.4 billion.

Lack of candor can create problems, as we have seen, but it also might be keeping you from opportunities. The economist Dr. Richard Thaler consulted with the extended leadership team of a company. He asked the executives if they would invest with a 50 percent chance of a $2 million profit and a 50 percent chance of a $1 million loss. Only three of the twenty-three executives in attendance raised their hands. In other words, the group proposed only three investments to the CEO, who happened to be sitting in the back of the room.

Thaler asked the CEO that if all of these projects were independent—that is, the success of one didn't impact others—how many of these theoretical initiatives would the CEO want to fund. His answer: all of them! "By taking on twenty-three projects, the firm expects to make $11.5 million with a chance of losing any money overall at less than 5 percent," the CEO quickly calculated.

"Well, that means you have a problem," Thaler replied. The experiment in the room said that his leadership team wasn't fully considering those opportunities or having the courage to advocate for them candidly. The CEO wasn't going to make $11.5 million off twenty-three projects, but only $1.5 million off three projects. If the executives in the room understood the company strategy, could calculate the expected values, and didn't think the CEO wanted to hear these ideas, the entire company was cheated out of the potential rewards.

"Data is only as good as our own biases," said Brenda Jin, founder of Bennu. "In order to truly find gaps and blind spots, leaders need to be as open to seeing those in the data as they are about finding them in their organizations." In order to lead change in organizations and implement decisions well, the organization and its leaders need to get real.

CULTIVATING CANDOR

"Successful leaders create an atmosphere of safety that permits spirited discussion, group learning, and trust. Candor is slightly different," explained Catherine Tinsley and Robin Dillon of Georgetown University and Peter Madsen from Brigham Young University. "It's a willingness to speak the unspeakable, to expose unfulfilled commitments, to air the conflicts that undermine apparent consensus." This has to be the expectation, not the exception, in order to implement decisions well.

"Candor means that people express their real opinions, not what they think team players are supposed to say," they continued. "Candor helps wipe out the silent lies and pocket vetoes that occur when people agree to things they have no intention of acting on. It prevents unnecessary rework and revisiting of decisions that sap productivity." Candor can kill the creosote bush before it poisons new ideas.

In her book, *Radical Candor*, Kim Scott talks about the importance of balancing two dimensions in feedback: you must care personally, and you must tell people when their work is and isn't good enough. Her research and experience at Google and Apple primarily focuses on feedback that managers give to employees, but truth travels the other direction as well. Everyone benefits when senior leaders are told how they can be better by someone who cares about them and the business.

Have you ever been in a presentation where, after an hour-long show of charts, graphs, and data, there is total silence in response to the speaker's final invitation for questions and feedback? This can happen in a written document review I described earlier, although it is much less common. "Everybody is waiting for the boss to speak," observed Balaji

Krishnamurthy, chairman of ThinkShift, in a recent interview. "They want to know which way the wind is blowing. Once the boss has established his or her position, there is a plethora of supporting comments. Everybody in the room seems to be aligned accordingly. Lo and behold, the group arrives at a consensus decision!" One can imagine that this is how those meetings at Quaker went before the Snapple acquisition.

This is why leaders should speak last. Author Simon Sinek explained that holding your opinions to yourself until everyone has spoken does two things. First, "it gives everybody else the feeling that they have been heard. It gives everyone else the ability to feel that they have contributed." And secondly and absolutely critical for truth seeking: "you get the benefit of hearing what everybody else has to think before you render your opinion."

If this is not common in your organization, you may have to call on others and tell the group that you are holding off your thoughts until the end to give others the encouragement to speak out first. You may be surprised that your team advocates for the things you were going to say, which serves as a third benefit of speaking last. It allows you to observe the calibration of the team to the strategy. If you also demonstrate the caring humanity that Scott recommends, you can help team members from feeling like they wasted their time expressing opinions when you already knew the "correct" answer.

It is important to note that this is the opposite advice and training that leaders received in their graduate or executive education courses where the smartest commentary got the best results. You have to be willing to place the organization and the decisions ahead of your ego.

ENCOURAGING IMPERFECTION

Alan Mulally took over a troubled Ford Motor Company as its CEO in 2006. His Kansas upbringing and thirty-seven years with Boeing had left him with a disarming manner, unwavering resolve, and a knack for team building. Exactly what a company that was losing $17 billion a year needed.

He implemented a business review every Thursday morning where his team would review color-coded progress charts. Anything on plan was green. Anything at risk was yellow. Anything off plan was red. He posted cultural values on the wall including, "people first," "everyone is included," "clear performance goals," "one plan," "find-a-way attitude," and "facts and data." Expectations were clear, or so he thought.

For several weeks in a row, all of the executive leadership showed charts that were all in green. Halfway through the third week's meeting, Mulally had seen enough. "We're going to lose billions of dollars this year," he interrupted. "Is there anything that is not going well here?" He was met with stone-cold silence.

In preparation for the meeting on the fourth week, Mark Fields, the head of Ford's operations in America, had a choice to make. His team had identified a problem with the new Ford Edge at an Ontario, Canada plant. The issue might have been an anomaly or something he could quickly fix without others noticing. Not mentioning it was the culture at Ford. Telling the truth and exposing challenges was a good way to lose your job. Perhaps after getting passed up for the CEO role, he felt he had nothing to lose. His report that week showed the goal for the Edge launch in red.

The room went quiet as everyone assumed Fields was as good as gone. Instead, Mulally started clapping and said, "Mark, that is great visibility." He turned to the group and asked,

"Who can help Mark with that?" The room went from shock to a flurry of offers of engineering support and information.

Mulally told Fields in the meeting, "You aren't red. The issue you're working on is red." That made an impression. Within a few weeks, the charts around the room had so much red, it was said, that the meeting looked like a crime scene. They were finally building trust.

This transparency, both at an individual level of vulnerability and visibility across the whole of the organization, helped Ford pull itself out of the ditch. They became the only American automobile manufacturer that didn't have to take Federal money during the recession of 2007 and 2008.

Gerry Perkel used to tell our sales teams at Planar that no one should ever lose a deal alone. If we lose, we lose, but at least we would have applied creative problem-solving and marshaled all the resources we could to win. The same goes for business problems and issues. Even in environments with great accountability, no leader should fail alone. It requires a kind of humility and trust of the team in order for people to parade their struggles and ask for help. However, the results are worth the awkwardness and risk.

ENSURING DEBATE

Abraham Lincoln has earned his reputation as one of the best leaders the White House has ever seen. In her biography of Lincoln, Pulitzer-prize-winning American historian, Doris Kearns Goodwin, details the men who served in his cabinet of advisors during the tumultuous Civil War era from 1861 to 1865 (later adapted for the film, *Lincoln*). She called it a "team of rivals," as it included several political opponents. I imagine there were many awkward and contentious moments with that group. In the end, these advisors helped Lincoln see his blind spots and led to a legacy which includes the 13th amendment to the US Constitution that abolished slavery.

Ever wonder where that phrase *devil's advocate* came from? The devil's advocate was a former official position in the Catholic Church, tasked with arguing *against* the conferring of sainthood on candidates in order to uncover character flaws or misrepresentation of the evidence. It is now a role played by leaders who ensure intellectual honesty in their peers or bosses. In the church, the role was also known as the "Promoter of the Faith," ironic in a way because their job was to dissent. They maintained the bar and upheld the standard. In order to build a lasting business, you need to have a diversity of counsel who play this dissenting role and who are the upholder of your brand.

Alfred Sloan was the CEO of General Motors and namesake of the business school at MIT. He believed in the power of dissenting options. In cases when his leadership team agreed, he would say: "I take it we are all in complete agreement on the decision here. Then I propose we postpone further discussion of the matter until our next meeting to give ourselves time to develop disagreement and perhaps gain some understanding of what the decision is all about." I challenge you to try that in your next meeting and require it for every one-way door decision.

FISHING WITH A NET

"It is very rare that those in positions of leadership get told the truth," agreed Josh Stump, President of Buckley Law who has spent over twenty years in the courtroom representing some of the biggest companies in the world. "Not only are facts withheld, but they lack a key feedback loop to their decision making."

Stump uses the example of a witness in a deposition to illustrate the point. A deposition is when a witness is called by the opposition to give testimony under oath prior to the trial. The idea is for the opposing lawyer to get as much information as possible about the other side's case. Meanwhile, the lawyer for the witness is trying to limit how much is shared. For that reason, they will advise the witness that the answer to the question of "Do you know the time?" is either "yes" or "no." The answer is never "four fifteen." Lawyers on both sides of the case are expected to fish from a line. They ask specific questions to get specific answers to uncover the truth, one fact at a time.

There are ways to help people tell the truth. Staying silent on your position and speaking last is one of them. Another is to create a space where someone feels like sharing freely. When those fail, the direct question can help.

Even if not under oath, "People are more willing to lie by omission than commission," observed Dr. Richard Thaler. "If I am selling you a used car, I do not feel obligated to mention that the car is burning a lot of oil, but if you ask me explicitly: 'Does this car burn a lot of oil?' you are likely to wrangle an admission from me that yes, there has been a small problem along those lines. To get at the truth, it helps to ask specific questions." Lawyers know this, which is why they conduct depositions and courtroom cross-examinations in this way.

But your next video conference or board meeting is not a deposition (at least, I hope not). You don't have to ask questions in this way.

Mediator Alexandra Carter talks about an epiphany she had on the beach watching fishermen. "I realized one of the reasons people tend to feel so stuck when asking questions is because, when we ask questions, we are fishing with a line rather than with a net—meaning, we are asking closed questions that give us very little and often unhelpful information."

In contrast, Carter finds that the questions that begin "tell me…" are the magic that "open up an entire world to your view." When leaders ask questions like "tell me what is going on here?" or "tell me why or why not something will work" or, even a simple, "tell me more," this can get the truth spilling out. Lawyers like to use this approach for opposing witnesses for this reason. For leaders, "tell me how I can be better at getting input" can be insightful. Depending on the culture in your company and the past experience of your employees and teammates, these open-ended questions might take some practice. There could be a reason people are only answering direct questions.

LOOK FOR THE OUTLIERS

Even if your colleagues do not mean to mislead, their own biases and the challenges of speaking up, when most people want to avoid conflict, can lead to bad or unhelpful information. This is true of all leaders. In order to avoid this, you need to keep your eyes and ears open.

One very telling source of truth is the anecdote. When you hear of a specific disappointed customer, missed shipment, manufacturing error, or execution miss, do not dismiss it as a one-off. Don't immediately go back to your overall customer satisfaction rating or quality reports and take them at face value. This particular situation could be the insight you have been looking for. "The thing I have noticed is that when the anecdotes and the data disagree, the anecdotes are usually right," Jeff Bezos observed. There may be "something wrong with the way you are measuring."

I remember learning about the power of the anecdote in high school debate. Decades after debating retirement security my senior year, I can still rattle off a list of horrific crimes that are committed against the elderly that I had memorized. I used this piece of anecdotal evidence in nearly every debate round. It did not include a single number or quantification. It didn't tell you how often the horrors occurred or the likelihood of these tragedies. The anecdote was from a respected source and painted a compelling picture. It didn't matter how often these things happened. Even once was too often. When pressed by my opponent debater as to how big of a problem it was, they would sound like an insensitive jerk. I would just refer back to the anecdote and call on our common humanity. This one paragraph of storytelling won me a lot of debate rounds.

This is true in business as well. If you say you are customer-obsessed and a single customer is let down, it is important to dive deeply to understand if it really was a fluke or some unaddressed process or policy issue that would benefit not only this customer, but many others. It could be your culture is falling out of calibration. Perhaps other customers, who aren't complaining, are just quietly leaving you for your competitors. Of course, businesses, development teams, and the like have to prioritize. Not all problems loom equally. But in order to prioritize, you need to understand the problem with a thorough investigation. It is precisely in these investigations that real progress is made to improve operations. It is not uncommon to uncover a big win from an easy fix. I have designed whole new product offerings inspired by an anecdote relayed by a customer service agent.

Even if nothing changes on a wide scale from these inquiries, you have had an opportunity to revisit the customer needs, your standards, and the risks. Research has shown that decision-makers may clearly understand the statistical risk represented by a deviation but grow increasingly less concerned. It is not just numbers and data that can help keep the organization and the team well-calibrated to the strategy: it is the stories.

REMAIN OPEN

You can implement opportunities for truth telling and try to build a culture of candor. Ultimately the success of these efforts falls to how the leader responds to surprising, disappointing, or infuriating information.

Michael Dell was ten years into his tenure as founder and CEO of the computer company bearing his name. The company was growing by 127 percent a year, and they had outstripped their ability to manage it effectively and experienced a cash-flow crisis—the kind of crisis that suffocates and kills businesses.

"We didn't fully understand the relationships between costs, revenues, and profits within the different parts of our business," Dell explained. "There were internal disagreements about which businesses were worthwhile and which were not." The problem of their quick growth was "that we had been over-enthusiastically pursuing every opportunity that presented itself." This led to them over-extending their management capacity, systems, and resources, like cash.

It was in this experience that Dell found there is an easy way to test whether he and his team were making decisions based on self-protecting emotions and taking the easy way out confirming their opinions. "When you come across data that is strikingly different from what you previously thought," he asked. "How long does it take for you to shift your thinking?" How do you react? Do you deny the data, or do you dig deeper? Dell concluded that the longer it took him personally to accept new data, the more he was relying on emotion or resting in his confirmation bias. And this approach was no longer working. He needed to hear things he didn't want to hear.

"One of the challenges you face as a company grows is that you tend to get a little too close to your own strengths and weaknesses, and it's hard to be objective," he observed. "I've heard this referred to as 'believing your own press,' but I prefer to think of it as 'breathing your own exhaust.' It doesn't sound healthy—because it isn't."

Dell and his board of directors brought in Bain & Company to develop the metrics that would guide the company into the future and inform its new operational processes. Kevin Rollins, who was the lead partner at Bain for Dell, joined Dell's executive team and went on to become the President and CEO. He was replaced by Dell again in 2007 amidst poor financial performance and criticism that Rollins wasn't open to feedback. It is true that even the most experienced and accomplished leaders need to be ever vigilant about not breathing their own exhaust.

I find that when receiving difficult feedback if I acknowledge the awkwardness, express gratitude, quiet my defensiveness, and follow-up on what I learned, I am more likely to receive it again. Proactively sharing examples of times when feedback changed you, is a great way to open a dialogue. Think back to the feedback you have given and received with grace, and I bet you see the same patterns. This is how to avoid "running businesses into the ground" and how to keep the planes in the air.

PRO TIPS:

- Don't breathe your own exhaust or believe your own press.
- Get outside perspectives.
- Fish with the net of open-ended questions.
- Speak last.
- Treat feedback as a gift, even if it is hard to receive. Remember, it was even harder to give.

CHAPTER 11:

ACTIONING TRUTH

___

"Anything mentionable is manageable."

—FRED ROGERS, MINISTER, AND TELEVISION
PERSONALITY, MR. ROGERS NEIGHBORHOOD

As Cinderella would agree, a new pair of shoes might just change your life.

When professional stylist Morgan Wider meets with a new client, they are often in the midst of an identity crisis. Making a dizzying number of decisions about their wardrobe can be overwhelming, so she rarely starts there. "My first call with a client might not even be about clothes," she explained to me in a recent interview. "I ask 'what do you want to be known for?'" This is important because then there is a reason to proceed. Her client feels decisions are necessary.

"Everyone is running from something," she continued. "The fear of letting go of a past decision. Fear that they won't be able to find anything better. Fear of uncertainty. Fear that change might leave them wondering who they are."

These same fears that emerge in Wider's conversations with clients in their closets apply to board room decisions, as well. Leaders all want to be known for something. And even experienced leaders can be shackled by the sunk costs of past decisions or anxiety about the future. It is easy to see how leaders can get paralyzed and sabotage their speed and success.

When her clients experience these fears, Wider suggests a first purchase: a pair of shoes. "The fit for your feet doesn't tend to be as loaded as the fit on other parts of the body, and because most people hold onto shoes for too long, even if it means their feet hurt or they are in bad repair, they are easier to let go of," she explained. "We build on that momentum to make other choices." A first step in a new pair of shoes can help break down the fear and begin a change.

Although I always advise a new pair of shoes as part of the solution, in all seriousness, this is good advice for any leader hoping to implement change, especially in the face of anticipated resistance. Find a part of your business where the thought of change isn't so "loaded," to use Wider's word. Start in a part of the business where the customer is no longer being served, or processes are out of date. Find a place where you can install a hinge and make a two-way door decision quickly. Using that success as an example, you can demystify the change and build positive momentum.

"It's an early win that becomes the first of many," Wider concluded. People may fear change, but who fears a new pair of shoes, after all?

There is a difference, however, between the paranoia that keeps you on your toes (pun intended—couldn't resist) and the fear that keeps you from facing choices and your organization objectively and putting that insight into action.

Balancing the tension between vulnerability and confidence is the art of leadership. On one side of the spectrum is the tenacity and resolve to hold tightly to convictions and thus build the confidence of the organization. Confidence is the winner's mindset we explored in previous chapters. On the other end is the willingness to be wrong, acknowledge you are wrong, and lead change. The leader walks the tightrope keeping these conflicting emotions in equilibrium. Once you face the truth about your business, you must action it.

KEEPING YOUR PERSPECTIVE FRESH

Economist Dr. Richard Thaler and psychologist Dr. Eldar Shafir conducted research among wine lovers asking for an estimate of the cost of a bottle of wine for which they paid $20 and could sell or replace for $75. The multiple-choice answers ranged from $0 (the reasoning being that they had already paid for it in the past) to $75 (the cost to buy a new one or the money lost when comparing drinking the bottle to selling it) and figures in between. Surprisingly, the most popular answer, which they put on the survey as a joke, was $55. "I get to drink a bottle that is worth $75 that I only paid $20 for, so I am saving money by drinking this bottle," was the faulty logic. This is the nonscientific answer that drives scientists to drink!

The original acquisition price is what economists would call a *sunk cost*. You can't recover it, and economists would say to ignore it in analysis. But that is easier said than done. It seems like a bad thing to have sunk cost into something. Some leaders can tie their ego or pride to sunk costs. Knowing how much you have invested or how gung-ho you were about that investment early on can blind you to the right path forward. It can become part of the creosote bush that squashes new ideas. You have to be willing to value the lessons you have learned along the way as a form of ROI.

In the fall of 1984, Intel's Andy Grove and Gordon Moore were facing a huge dilemma. Their memory chip business was unsuccessfully competing with Japanese producers who offered lower-price and higher-quality products. They couldn't cut production fast enough to outpace the falling demand. "We had meetings and more meetings, bickering, and arguments, resulting in nothing but conflicting proposals," Grove recalled. The debates continued during that grim and frustrating year until they had a moment of clarity.

He looked out the windows of his office in Santa Clara, California, at the Ferris wheel of the Great American amusement park. He saw the ride revolving in the distance in a never-ending, futile circle.

He turned back to Moore and asked, "If we got kicked out and the board brought in a new CEO, what do you think he would do?"

Without hesitation, Moore answered, "He would get us out of memories."

"I stared at him numb," Grove recalled. "Then I said, 'Why shouldn't you and I walk out of the door, come back and do it ourselves?'" They had let the debate revolve for over a year. They had an emotional and financial investment in the memory business that was hard to let go of, but now with perspective, they were ready to make a change. They got off the wheel. They could start implementing the decision.

PLANNING ACTION

Chris Curtin served as Visa's chief brand and innovation marketing officer and has seen his share of high-stakes decision making. "If you want to align teams to focus on execution," he observed in a recent interview, "the big unlock is to get people to agree, not just on the goals, but also the assumptions around the goals." Buy-in requires more than just nodding in agreement. It requires a common understanding of the water in which you are swimming. It requires the sorting of fears from facts. "You always need to ask, 'What would it take to hit that goal?' That is the only way you know you really have a plan and not just wishful thinking."

To avoid wishful thinking or false impressions of alignment, Curtin recommends premortems. These are meetings that you have ahead of the action to ask and answer why the decision will be successful or fail. This meeting is where you get all the worst-case scenarios out on the table and have the functional experts weigh in. "Ask the group to brainstorm all the reasons why a miss would occur," he explained. "Would it be because you're missing the right sales materials, running the wrong promotions, setting the wrong price, missing a market window? Pretend you have a crystal ball."

"Postmortems, or post-action reporting, don't do you any good," Curtin continued. They are useful for descriptive or diagnostic analysis alone. "You can't change the view in the rear-view mirror. But premortems can change the future." Premortem discussions can move you to predictive or prescriptive analysis, as Gartner has defined in their Analytics Ascendency Model.

These meetings have another advantage: cross-functional buy-in. "Postmortems put people on the defensive," Curtin observes. Since results have already occurred, the analysis has consequences and can lead to finger-pointing, especially if the miss leads to a crisis. "Premortems allow the staff to be more creative and to share the potential problems before they occur. Plans developed in isolation, with the hope that they can reconcile after the fact, never work."

This has now become a standard part of my annual planning processes or major product launches with my team. We take our operating plan for the year and brainstorm as a team why we will be successful and what might come off target, and why. This has led to very interesting insights. The candor helps to identify areas you need to watch, and if something does slip, you already have a language and a common understanding of what you are going to do. All in all, this approach helps the team have the best chance of success at the start and throughout the implementation of a decision. It is a mechanism to minimize risk.

Curtin was with Disney when they went into the cruise business. He recalls that people would ask him whether Disney-themed cruises would siphon off foot traffic in the parks. Same when Disney started offering guided tours. Skeptics asked, "How are you sure that the tours will have the same quality and entertainment level as the parks?" These are logical questions that good businesspeople should ask when reviewing a product portfolio. "The only way to address them was not to hide from or run away from those risks, but to run toward them," Curtin said. He found "The more you talk about risk publicly, you reduce the chances of that risk occurring." Confidence builds in collaboration.

In his TED Talk, now with over nine million views, author and investor Tim Ferris shared a technique he uses in business and in life which takes this a step further. He calls it *fear setting*. If goal setting is about writing down what you want to happen, fear setting is the opposite: writing down what you don't want. He breaks the analysis into three columns: 1) Define: you write out the worst things that you can imagine might come from a decision or circumstance; 2) Prevent: write down what you could do to prevent those worst things from happening; and finally, 3) Repair: what you could do to recover if one of these things occurred.

"I can trace all of my biggest wins and all of my biggest disasters averted back to doing fear-setting at least once a quarter," Ferris added.

A team can create an overwhelming number of worst-case scenario ideas in these exercises, especially if you truly learned lessons from past failures and are applying them afresh. You may find, like Ferris, that some of your fears are very well-founded. When this happens, Curtin reminds that "Your job isn't to solve all the world's problems, but to produce something that the customer finds valuable." Focusing back on your customer obsession can be the first step to clarity and a shared sense of prioritization.

RETHINKING

As we have discussed, some leaders have a self-preservation response to the idea of being wrong, and it can slow them down and cause them to make a poor decision. But what happens if things do start to go poorly as implementation begins? What if you seek out and receive truth, and it isn't what you want to hear? Before you can implement the mitigation plans you devised in the premortem discussions, you have to move the reaction from your heart to your head.

Some leaders will go through the entire five stages of grief, passing denial, anger, depression, and bargaining before they arrive at acceptance. I have seen leaders and been a leader who has fallen victim to this cycle. Research shows that if being wrong runs counter to a leader's beliefs about themselves, corrections can be ineffective. So much so that it can trigger confirmation bias and shut down well-meaning feedback and input that you need to be successful as a leader. As we already established, not being told the truth is akin to death by exposure for your business. If the measure of a decision is in its successful implementation, one must remain open to being wrong on the way to making it right.

Wharton business school professor and best-selling author, Adam Grant tackled this subject in his book, *Think Again*. "When people reflect on what it takes to be mentally fit, the first idea that comes to mind is usually intelligence. The smarter you are, the more complex the problems you can solve—and the faster you can solve them," he explains. "Intelligence is traditionally viewed as the ability to think and learn. Yet in a turbulent world, there's another set of cognitive skills that might matter more: the ability to rethink and unlearn." Unlearning requires commitment and a willingness to move forward with new information and let it change us.

I am told that my brother-in-law learned to run before he learned to walk. Whenever he was about to fall, he just changed directions and kept going. A fast pivot followed every wobble. You can keep moving forward if you keep moving and responding to the environment in which you find yourself.

What can stop leaders from moving forward? When fear turns to shame. Instead of treating mistakes or poor performance as actions that went wrong, which might produce a feeling of guilt, we can view missteps as evidence that we are bad people producing feelings of shame. "If you think you're a bad person, that's a much harder thought to counteract, and that might lead you to withdraw from other people," says Taya Cohen from Carnegie Mellon University. The same people who could tell you the truth and get you back on track.

Leaders might ask themselves, "If I make a mistake, if I fail, how does that affect who I am and how I see myself, as well as how others see me?" Cohen continued. To process failure in a healthy way or even fully consider the possibility of failure in order to mitigate risks, we must put it in context and "recognize that there's a learning opportunity in every failure." It's a long race. You just have to keep running believing a win is possible.

Susan Wojcicki demonstrated this well when she led Google Videos, which came out right before YouTube. "We quickly realized that YouTube was generating a lot more traffic, and it was more popular," she recalled. In 2006, Google bought YouTube, which was still an unprofitable start-up. "It's very hard when you build a product to admit that there's this other product that's better—and you're going to pay $1.65 billion for it," she added. "The lesson I learned was that when you make a mistake, admit it as soon as possible. If you keep trying to fix it, you might miss your opportunity to make it better for the long term."

"When failure occurs, sift through it for any lessons to be learned," advised Art Gensler, the architect and namesake founder of the global architecture firm Gensler. "Too many people dwell on the past, and they burn up precious energy that could be otherwise invested in moving on and finding new opportunities. Put your energy into looking forward."

I once heard a fable about a city and a town separated by a mountain. In order to facilitate trade, both local governments decided that the long and treacherous road around the mountain, which was the only route available to merchants and travelers, needed to be replaced by a tunnel. The team from the city began work by hiring an engineering crew who surveyed the mountain, took soil samples, and created an extensive project plan showing all the work that needed to be done by when, by whom to build a high-quality tunnel. Gantt charts were created and vendors evaluated.

On the opposite side of the mountain, the town's leaders observed and rejected the city's approach. Not wasting any time, they assembled two drilling operations and put them on either side of the mountain, and asked them to begin digging right away with the information they had.

The expert engineers from the city mocked the drillers in action. "How do you know if the two teams will even meet up in the middle?" they would ask. To which the town's project leaders replied, "Well, if they don't, then we will have two tunnels." If one tunnel was good, then two might be better.

Just like there was more than one way to approach tunnel building, there are multiple ways for your organization to successfully implement decisions. The key is knowing what to hold fast to and what is negotiable.

It took courage for Wojcicki to say that her pet project was not as good as YouTube. It would be like the city in our fable abandoning their tunnel-building efforts and investing in the town's drilling approach. It was hard for Grove and Moore to get out of memories after holding on so long. You can't be numb or ignore the risks of your decisions. The fabled city planners could have beat themselves up for some unforeseen issue, or the town's drillers could have hit bedrock and had to come back with the city with their broken drill bits. But as we have seen, if you can mention the risks ahead of time, you can manage them. Uncertainty is certain. But your written plan to obsess about customers can provide a north star, and the premortem can give you a contingency plan. And if all else fails, you have a great pair of new shoes and confidence that you can keep going.

PRO TIPS:

- Do the equivalent of buying a new pair of shoes in your business and get an early win.
- Try to imagine what others would do in your situation unfettered by the past or too much knowledge.
- Conduct premortems and fear setting. Reduce risk by talking about failure ahead of time.
- Don't be afraid to be wrong along the way. The current setback might be on the path to success.

CHAPTER 12:

COMMITTING COURAGEOUSLY

———

"You may have to fight a battle more than once to win it."

—BARONESS MARGARET THATCHER, GREAT
BRITAIN'S FIRST FEMALE PRIME MINISTER

An implementation is an act of courage. Commitment to the results of decisions requires saying "yes." Saying "yes" begins unintuitively with saying "no."

I am an optimist and a high-productivity person, so it requires discipline for me to say "no" to a great idea. Others I work with do not suffer from this, and I rely on them for a rational word of caution or a well-placed question about priority, just like they rely on me for energy and a "why not now?" bias. Good plans executed well require both.

In business planning, one of the most important decisions to be made is what is not going to get done. Jim Collins, the business advisor and author of *Good to Great*, advised leaders to make a "stop doing list" alongside their "to do" lists. We learned earlier that Dell was saying "yes" too often, and it nearly put them out of business. The same might be happening in your organization if the cost bubble of implementing yesterday's decisions overlaps too much with your plans for the future.

When pursuing a strategy, one must ask what are we giving up to take this path of action? What do we need to stop doing?

WHAT YOU LEARN BY SAYING "NO"

When Kat Cole joined as the president of Cinnabon, she knew she had her work cut out for her. She also knew that her leadership was not going to give her more money to invest in innovation. She had to be scrappy and find savings within the business to invest in these new initiatives.

"I did nothing for the first 60 days essentially other than work in what we call our 'bakeries,' our franchise locations. I rolled cinnamon rolls. I took out the trash," Cole explained. "And I'm not talking shaking hands and kissing babies. I was there for hours learning, listening, watching, asking questions." It was hands-on research.

Her first question was, "What do we throw away?" Having spent a career in restaurants, she knew that the waste in the business model started in the wastebasket. "So if we're paying people to do things or spending time on things or putting products into stores that aren't going to work for us, let's stop," she told her team.

In my experience, it is easier for an outsider to see opportunities for simplification or savings than others who might have gotten used to the way things are. I used to joke with new employees approaching their ninety-day anniversary that they would soon lose all of their perspective, so now was the time to be brutally honest and ask the "Why are we doing this?"

questions. Through these conversations, I have found opportunities to streamline approvals, reduce the manual steps of processes, eliminate projects, stop running reports, create new reports, and generally found ways to do more with less.

The second question Cole asked is the opposite: "When do we say 'no'?"

"That question is about missed opportunities," she explained. "When do we say 'no' to employees? When do we say 'no' to customers? And there were very clear themes to those answers," she recalled. As we have explored, I have grown a deep and abiding appreciation for customer verbatims. Customers who talk about their poor experience on a website or with a product can provide a shortcut to breakthroughs. Those anecdotal insights can lead to gold as we've discussed.

Finally, Cole asked a third question: "If you were me, the president of the company, what is one thing you would do differently to make this business better?" She found that those closest to the action have insights they have probably been dying to share if they had only been asked. Much like the premortem we described earlier, soliciting subject-matter expertise can provide useful input. It was from these insights that Cole built her innovation plans and found the funding to make them happen.

DON'T BLINK

"Making the right decision is one thing. Driving that decision forward is another," said Martyn Etherington, the chief marketing officer of Teradata, in a recent interview. If employees don't know where you are going and are empowered to say "no" or slow decisions down, you can cause initiatives to fail.

"You can agree and commit to a decision. That is easy," he observed. "You can disagree and commit. But you can't agree and not commit," Etherington continued. "That is cancer and kills teamwork. Your organization needs to have the vocabulary of commitment."

Etherington recalled when he was with a leading business communications provider and "the chairman, was very wedded to the company name. However, in my role, I was getting a different picture." He went on to say that customers, analysts, and influencers were telling him that "the brand was not relevant, old-fashioned, and associated with legacy."

"Doing nothing was not an option," he contended. "We had to address our perception as being relevant as a cloud company." He had to build a business case beginning and ending with the customer.

Everything was on the table, from the company name, their brand promise and positioning, and how the sales teams communicated a contemporary customer-centric brand onto the market. "We tested everything with our customers," Etherington recalled. "In parallel, we communicated, educated, and involved our employees throughout the process."

Etherington was eventually advised to speak directly to the board of directors without the CEO's endorsement. "I brought in market data, the customer research, and I asked for their support. Even if they didn't agree, I asked that they not derail. In the end, six of the directors supported, and three abstained, and we moved forward." He could have let the CEO's wavering support or the chairman's commitment to the old brand cause him to lose conviction. But in the end, he acted with courage.

"Being courageous is not being reckless," he added. "It is holding both a conviction and a growth mindset." That balance of confidence and openness proved critical in the next steps of implementation. Moreover, it was the voice of the customer and company alignment that helped convince the chairman that a rebrand was the right thing to do for the company, shareholders, and customers.

In my experience, leaders must hold the confidence of their teams until those teams see the picture clearly, through the lens of their customers, and can implement it on their own. There will always be naysayers. You can't ignore criticism or feedback, and in fact, you need it to lead, but you must channel it. You can't blink on what is critical. You must be willing to judge yourself and your decisions through the lens of the customer to stay calibrated to the true north. If you find that what you were holding as "true north" is no longer reflecting the real, durable needs of the customer, then you need to be willing to change.

KEEP THE CUSTOMER IN FOCUS

Brent Michael joined EverCommerce in August 2020 to run two of their portfolio companies, Allmeds and iSalus Healthcare, which serve the electronic medical records (EMR) and practice management market. The previous leader had made the decision, just seven months earlier, to end support for Allmeds, a legacy platform, and transition their physician practice customers to iSalus.

It seemed like a great way to reduce operating costs, improve service, and provide a better product to customers at the time. The problem is that customers didn't see it that way. Following that announcement, Allmeds lost 30 percent of their customers and 40 percent of the revenue. Customer attrition was dramatic.

It was no secret that the entire healthcare IT industry was modernizing to cloud-based solutions. "Everyone in the industry knew that physician practices would be forced to go at some point," Michael offered in a recent interview. "But we didn't let customers make the decision on their own. Or at least we didn't guide them based on a 'why do something, why now, why us' decision process. We just forced a decision that meant dramatic change for these practices. They didn't see the value."

"What I have learned in my 30 years of working with customers is that if you put a gun to their head and tell them to do something, it is not going to go well," Michael explained provocatively. "You may get the answer you want the very second you ask the question," he added, "but they'll never forget that you pointed the gun in the first place, and their subsequent actions will reflect that."

He partnered with his new chief financial officer to put together a fresh analysis of the business, centered around a new set of metrics: revenue and cost per physician. The aim was to figure out what was best for the customer long-term.

"The analysis showed how much we were giving up with the decision we were implementing," he observed. "There had been an assumption that the cost of maintaining AllMeds was very high, but that was simply not true. The cost of transitioning customers, for free, to iSalus was substantially more than anticipated once you factored in the data migration, training, and overall disruption to the implementation team." By looking at the business by physician, not by practice, they found that they were actually making more money by keeping Allmeds. And, more importantly, they could retain the clients and all the recurring revenue that those clients brought.

He got feedback from all levels of the company and directly from customers. He found the story consistent. So, Michael made the hard decision to pivot. To stay true to the commitment to the customer, but to execute it in a very different way. He drafted a letter to all customers just a few weeks after taking the reins. "It said that there was a new focus on the client experience, and that they could stay on the software as long as we could support it," Michael recalled.

A copy of the letter was sent to every employee, explaining the shift, the strategy, and the vision of creating a world-class customer experience. He was implementing loudly. "This was music to their ears," he said. Frontline staff said that it was what the customer wanted all along. To implement the change, they shifted support staff that knew the product back into positions where they could help customers.

The response from customers was one of gratitude. Some still wanted to transition, and others were going to take their time and work with EverCommerce to find the right solution. "The message we are now delivering allows customers to feel like they're a part of the process," he said.

Michael holds weekly meetings with this leadership team and quarterly town halls for all 150 employees to learn how the strategy is working. They utilize an Objectives and Key Results (OKR) structure throughout EverCommerce that forces employees on what moves the needle and gives broader visibility through the company's strategy implementation. "Employees are finding new ways to contribute and have an impact on the combined entity because we honored what was good about what they had built," he added.

So whether the decision is big or small, the process of implementation is the same. "You are never going to make everyone happy, but if you can defend, show, and explain the decision and show forward progress, you have a better chance of success," Michael concluded. It is only with an unwavering focus on the customer that you make sure you stay on course.

BE OPEN (NOT ON EVERYTHING,
BUT WHAT'S MOST IMPORTANT)

Michael Hyter is the president and CEO of The Executive Leadership Council and spoke about the importance of knowing what you want and letting that lead you in your career in his book *The Power of Choice.*

"You have to be clear about the outcome you want before you try to influence a situation," he wrote. "You have to know the goal you're moving toward in order to gauge whether you're having an impact—and where you are willing to negotiate. Be open to the possibility that there are likely several ways to achieve your goal, not just the solution you have in mind." He continued by saying that one must "be willing to back up or take some detours when you need to but stay focused on your desired outcome."

Some call this being stubborn about the vision but flexible on the details. Hyter was talking about career choices, but it applies more broadly to decisions that businesses make.

Consider Burbn. Named after founder Kevin Systrom's love of Kentucky whiskey, the Burbn app allowed a user to earn points for hanging out with friends or posting pictures of meet-ups. He and fellow programmer, Mike Krieger, analyzed customer usage and found that people weren't using the check-in features. Instead, "they were posting and sharing photos like crazy."

They were honest about the data, focused on photo-sharing, and scraped everything else. After a month of experimentation and prototyping, they launched a new app called "Instagram" in 2010. Two years later, the company, along with its eleven employees, was sold to Facebook for $1 billion in cash and stock. At the time the company had thirty million users and zero revenue. Five years later, the app has 600 million users and boasts a multi-billion-dollar ad business.

Similarly, after flailing around in a nascent market for podcasts in 2005, a San Francisco-based start-up called Odeo launched a short messaging service (SMS) for groups. They called their little side project, Twttr. Within six months of launch, Twttr had become Twitter, and the world was learning to communicate in 140-character posts.

I attended the SXSW digital conference in 2014 and Twitter cofounder, Biz Stone, took the stage and recalled those heady days when they "ruled SXSW" at their launch just seven years earlier. He told the story of someone who was in a bar and wanted to talk about work, but it was too loud. He tweeted that they should all go to another place, and by the time he got to the pub, there was already a queue outside the door. It was then he knew how powerful the platform could be. It was changing the movement of crowds in Austin, Texas, during a busy industry event. What else could it do?

Twitter has since been used to raise awareness of political topics, spread messages and movements, change celebrity culture, make the connection between brands and their customers more direct, democratize news reporting, and provide a rich data source for social scientists to conduct research. All of these things were never envisioned when Jack Dorsey sent the first tweet, which read: "just setting up my twttr" in 2006. This tweet was sold as a nonfungible token (NFT) for $2.9 million in 2021, something else not imagined in 2007 when Twitter was getting restarted.

These accomplishments would have never happened if the founders hadn't shown that flexibility that Hyter advised. Focusing on the customer and looking honestly at the data, they could be flexible on the path to get there.

BELIEVE SOMETHING BETTER AWAITS

Estée Lauder started her cosmetic company during the Great Depression. Despite the poor economy, the energetic Lauder said, "Women will open their purses for quality." This was illustrated later when her son would coin the idea of a "lipstick index," whereby lipstick sales went up during the 2001 recession, indicating women's willingness to spend on affordable luxuries.

Early on, she liked to say that before television, there were three forms of mass communication: telephone, telegraph, and tell-a-woman. She relied on the latter, growing her business through a network of salons around her home in New York and Florida, where she would travel each winter to "fiddle with women's faces." This approach played well to her endless energy and enthusiasm for beauty and fashion.

After the war, the booming economy and growing financial means among women helped Lauder secure relationships with Saks Fifth Avenue in New York and other boutique retailers around the country. These posh cosmetic counters added cache to her evolving brand, which had grown from home-printed labels to the signature blue-green packaging still used today.

By 1950, multi-million-dollar cosmetic companies like Coty and Revlon were routinely allocating between twenty and twenty-five of their net sales to advertising. Lauder and her husband and operations leader, Joe, had "scraped together the staggering—to them—sum of $50,000 for an advertising campaign and made an appointment with Madison Avenue heavy hitter Batten, Barton, Durstine, and Osborne," noted her son and future CEO of Estee Lauder Cosmetics, Leonard Lauder. The agency, that now goes by the abbreviation BBDO, told them that without a million-dollar budget, they could not run a campaign.

Much like we have seen with other leaders in this book, "that rejection turned out to be a gift from divine providence," noted Mr. Lauder. His mom went back to her "tell-a-woman" strategy. It was in her mind that this was "the most honest way to do business."

They took the $50,000 advertising budget they had saved (roughly $540,000 in today's dollars) and bought samples to give away. In one of the first examples of direct mail advertising, they sent a notice to every woman with charge accounts with their retail partners to get a free sample of face powder (in those days, charge accounts were with the store, as Visa and Mastercard had not created nationwide or global credit networks). The approach worked.

"Women trooped in to get the free sample, liked the product, and came back two months later to buy it," Lauder continued. "Meanwhile, just as we hoped, they told all their friends."

If they had been able to invest in an advertising campaign, like their competitors, they wouldn't have innovated their approach. "The giveaways created an opportunity to exercise the high-touch Estée Lauder sales approach, encourage spontaneous buying, increase loyalty among existing customers, and bring in new ones," Lauder concluded. It is still part of the strategy the brand uses seventy years later.

STAY THE COURSE AND STAY ALERT

To maintain flexibility and conviction can be a delicate balance. To maintain a vision and sort through the noise of day-to-day criticism can be a challenge. As we discussed earlier, Pinterest stayed the course, and it has paid off. Burbn pivoted and profited.

To strike a balance, Balaji Krishnamurthy advises "appointing an independent auditor, not involved in the decision, and provide them a few observable, measurable parameters baked into your decision." These assumptions could be factors related to economic growth, the size of the market, the needs of customers, or the movement of competitors. Things that you noted in your premortem or reflect the water you are swimming in today. Anything that can be objectively monitored or measured can be audited.

"Note your assumptions, and when the auditor finds something outside of the threshold, they ring a bell, and you reexamine the decision," he said. "As long as the assumptions hold true, so can your decision." This approach can help you right-size risk by having a process of re-evaluation that doesn't prevent you from focusing on exceptional execution.

This is the approach that my product management team at Planar used. At the time when we approved product development proposals, we set a *boundary box* around key business assumptions—proposed average selling price, bill-of-materials costs, marketing expenses, and development costs, to name a few. Then as the development continued, we revisited the boundaries to see if we were still in scope or if other decisions were warranted.

"No single decision is by itself," Krishnamurthy continued. "Sure, picking numbers for your lottery tickets are either right or wrong. Most business decisions are not like that." There are always multiple factors at play—some within your control and others out of your scope of influence—that contribute to whether a decision is viewed in hindsight as a winner. If you can set the course but remain alert, you can make large and small course corrections along the way to your end goals.

"It is hard to call any single decision right or wrong. It is more important to make a decision right than to make a right decision," Krishnamurthy concluded. "Your organization has to accept the notion of *making* a decision right."

PRO TIPS:
- Make a "not to do" list.
- Stay confident in your defendable decisions. Others are watching.
- Keep your customers in focus by learning your business from the ground up.
- Stay open to good surprises.
- Stay alert and make sure you hold fast to the things that are worth holding on to and you are being flexible with everything else.
- Appoint an auditor and document your assumptions to keep yourself accountable.

CHAPTER 13:

IMPLEMENTING LOUDLY

———

"Story is a sense-making device."

—MIKE MCHARGUE, AUTHOR, PODCAST HOST,
CONSULTANT, AND PUBLIC EDUCATOR

It was a sunny day in Palo Alto, California, and Netflix founder Reed Hastings met up with his head of business development, Delly Tamer, at a coffee shop. As Tamer told me in a recent interview, it was a year into the new company that now boasted thirty-five employees.

"We are considering eliminating DVD sales to focus on rentals and streaming. I'd like your opinion before I make a final decision," Hastings told Tamer.

Stunned, Tamer asked, "Wait, aren't DVD sales about 95 percent of our revenues?"

Ever precise, Hastings replied, "Ninety-seven percent." Tamer's jaw dropped.

It is easy to see the wisdom in this decision now, but when Netflix changed their business model to streaming, they hadn't proved it could be done, and they put nearly all of their revenue at stake.

After some time debating the impact of this decision on revenue, employees, and their ability to raise additional venture capital, Hastings made the decision. The DVD rental business was over.

"Immediately, I took out a paper pad from my backpack, set it on the table, and said, 'Okay, Reed. How do we execute?'," Tamer recalled. The debate was over. Now it was time to commit like Martyn Etherington spoke about in the last chapter.

"Wait, just like that?" Hastings said with shock. "You are ready to go along with this decision? You were so passionate about why we should not do that."

"I greatly appreciated being able to voice my opinion, but it was his final call," Tamer recounted. "My job is to follow to the letter. We all needed to move in the same direction." The decision was crystal clear, so the implementation began. And that implementation began with communication and action.

The key to alignment from the first idea throughout implementation is communication: clear, early, and often. To make the strategy heard, you must implement it loudly.

It would take eight years for streaming to become a reality in late 2006. "In my opinion, Reed Hastings's single biggest accomplishment at Netflix in the past twenty-two years wasn't the decision to move to streaming," Tamer recounted. "It was his multi-year perseverance at launching streaming against all odds without ever wavering." That, "was the best business decision he ever made." And like so many decisions I have recounted in this book, it wasn't a single decision. It was a series of decisions that made the difference.

You see, Hastings and his fledgling team at Netflix faced enormous pressure. Tamer recalled the day that Walmart announced it was getting into the DVD rental business. Netflix had gone public earlier that year at $15, and with this announcement, was trading at half of that. The stock market shuttered, and investors feared the worst.

Netflix didn't flinch and continued to build their subscriber base responding to press inquiries with this message of optimism: "We're glad to see them enter the market. They'll convince consumers that this is a cool new way to rent, and that will benefit Netflix." And less than two years later, in what the press called a "DVD rental truce," Walmart struck a deal, and Netflix took over their rental business. NetFlix now trades for 500x the IPO strike price.

Culture and talent density continue to play a role, even deep into implementation. "If there had been no trust in leadership, people would have abandoned ship," Tamer said. "They would have said 'I don't buy it,' and there would have been more pressure. I could honestly tell employees, 'I love this company, and I think we are awesome and are going to survive', and that helped build confidence." The faith in leadership and in the strategy built resilience into the organization for the long haul.

"It honestly wasn't until 2007 that the decision to pursue streaming seemed like a good one," Tamer recalled. The fact that it was hard and took a long time was difficult but had its benefits to the ever-optimistic Tamer. "If anyone could get into streaming in six or eight weeks, it would be imitated very easily," inviting more competition and pressure of other sorts. Instead, they enjoyed the benefit of competitive barriers. They created a fork in the road and made it harder for everyone else to follow their path. But this only occurred because of how Netflix implemented the decision over the years and how they committed to communication.

"Making sure that people know your decision is critical. What could kill a great decision is a lack of transparency. If people don't understand, they can't support," Tamer said.

Someone once told me rightly that "No one speculates that anything good is going on behind closed office doors." I have found that to be true. Employees or other stakeholders will just fill in the blanks and likely they are filling it in with their wildest imaginations about the worst things that could happen. Tamer added that consistent, clear communications could make all the difference, especially when you are asking teams to innovate for the long-term.

"Imagine that you invented a device that can record my memories, my dreams, my ideas, and transmit them to your brain. That would be a game-changing technology, right?" asked neuroscientist Uri Hasson in his TED Talk. "But in fact, he continued, "we already possess this device, and it's called the human communication system and effective storytelling,"

He went on to explain that our imagination is so powerful that a strong, compelling story will create an experience in our brain that is similar to having "an audiovisual experience and memory reinstatement." Stories are like the application programming interface (API) between our brains. Communication expert Mike McHargue says that stories are the most powerful tool we can use to organize information so that people don't have to burn very many calories to get our meaning. Stories help others get into the brain behind the decision we make as leaders. Ultimately, those visions are made real.

Here are some storytelling approaches that have worked for me and that might be useful in your implementations.

ACT IT OUT

A story can become a memory. And memories are what make up our identity as an organization and as individuals. Stories give things context and meaning. And this identity is what shapes culture over time. Stories are told and acted out. Like Jim Hurd sleeping in the sauna, we all have an opportunity to demonstrate the culture in acts of symbolism.

When I was with Leyard, I spent some marketing budget to redo the lobby of our small field office in Chicago. I knew we hosted customers in this office, and previously it had felt as warm as a warehouse. After a day of meetings, I drove a rented minivan to HomeGoods and bought a few chairs, tables, shelves, and wall art. I shut down several stores and packed the van to where the door barely closed. Back at the office the next morning, work began. I hung the new things alongside some framed product awards I had packed in my suitcase. I felt pretty silly, I must say, as the CMO of the company hanging shelves and potting plants in the office that morning, but I considered it a physical act of service to our employees and our brand. Employees responded very warmly, and it built stronger relationships. In a similar spirit, I have heard of executives giving up their offices to create team rooms for key projects or sending notes to employees praised in customer reviews. These acts of symbolism are important storytelling devices that help leaders lead.

It sounds so simple, but if you want your employees to take time off against your new vacation policy, you must yourself take a vacation. And tell people about your coming vacation. Set your out of office. And show people pictures of your vacation when you return. You must make it okay for them to implement the decision you intend.

The same goes for other decisions. If you want the organization to make use data, start asking questions about reports you receive or referencing data when you announce decisions. If you want to show your commitment to a new market, hold your next customer meeting in that country and give your presentation in the local language.

MAKE IT CONTAGIOUS

Jonah Berger, the best-selling author, describes why things catch on in his book, *Contagious*. He says that ideas that spread are things that make the person sharing them look good, are easily triggered by the environment, are laden with emotion, are public, and are practical. Content that meets these criteria travels speedily on the wheels of a story. I have seen these characteristics apply in the negative when damaging office gossip spreads like wildfire. I have also seen these same characteristics of story help socialize change, celebrate alignment, and make it popular to implement decisions and implement them well.

In an example of public, practical, and emotional decision implementation, Heidi Voorhees Haneberg was the chief operating officer at AVIXA when they pivoted their annual conference and tradeshow, InfoComm, to a virtual platform in 2020 in response to the COVID-19 pandemic. Once the decision was made and having only nine weeks to prepare, the organization broke into small agile teams to make it happen. The goal and the behavior change necessary to accomplish that goal spread quickly.

"We had to tell everyone to put their ego away," she explained in a recent interview. "If something is happening in which you are not involved," she told her staff, "just focus on what you're supposed to be doing." This was made possible with very clear storytelling. "There were so many moving pieces and parts. We were communicating all the time about challenges, pivots, new ideas," she continued. "In those nine weeks where everyone was so focused and dedicated, everyone on those teams worked their butt off, and they loved it," she recalled. "They were all working toward a common goal. There was clarity. There was strong communication." She described how traditionally siloed functional walls came down, ownership was shared, and there was urgency. This is what happens when communication meets up with a common, public purpose. It shouldn't take a pandemic to rally your team to implement change. You can create meaningful urgency by focusing on and amplifying customer needs.

SAY IT AGAIN (AND AGAIN, AND AGAIN, AND AGAIN)

The big myth about marketing leaders, or those in corporate communications roles, is that they are creative. Many of them are; but in reality, the most successful communicators—especially those tasked with change management—are doing it right when they make things, well, boring.

Even back in 1885, publisher Thomas Smith described that it took twenty times seeing an ad for a person to buy the product advertised. Back then, there were so many fewer messages and ways of communicating. Forrester tells its clients that today it can take up to twenty-seven interactions for a business buyer to make a decision. The same is true of internal communications to your employees or customer communications you want to send related to a decision or a change.

The first four times people are told about a decision, unless it is really big and impactful to their immediate work, they might not see it at all. By the seventh or eighth time, they are thinking "this old thing again." It has already become commonplace. The brand name or the main message has already embedded. Hopefully, all along the way, the message itself was simple, and the value proposition was compelling. But still, you might not see any results or changed behaviors.

By the time you reach the twelfth or thirteenth time, then things really start changing. *Awareness* turns to *Desire*, to use the words from PROSCI and their foundational work on change management. People are not just aware of it, they want to be a part. Now, you are getting somewhere. And by the time your employees hear about the change the sixteenth time, they accept it, and by the seventeenth or eighteenth, they are changing in response.

This means that leaders are in the business of mind-numbing repetition. That is how they do their job. This is how they become the culture officers they need to be. They say the same thing, over and over, across different mediums, until their target audience not only receives, but is transformed by the message. Anyone in the business of implementing decisions needs to drive toward being utterly and entirely tired of hearing about why the decision is good and worthy. Until they are so tired of it that they want to gouge their ears out, *only then* will their employees believe they have heard it at all. If you have ever led a big change initiative, you know exactly what I mean. It is shocking how often you have to communicate the same message to break through the noise.

MAKE IT FUN

Just because it is repetitive doesn't mean it has to be dull. Dr. Cass Sunstein, the Harvard professor and author of forty books, describes that in order for things to be engaging, they need to be easy, attractive, social, and timely. And he added to this standard list a new requirement: fun.

"The word *fun* connotes something that makes you smile with a kind of ease and joy," he explained. "The notion of fun is associated with play." Change initiatives and big corporate executions often are missing an element of delight. Change might be necessary. It might be inevitable. You might talk about it ad nauseum. But is it ever fun? At the level that the execution is taking place, you are more likely to find a mix of unrelenting deadlines, forced compliance, and empty platitudes.

Cass quoted the political writer Emma Goldman who said, "I will participate in no revolution in which they do not dance" (which is quite a statement for an anarchist, I must say). Any big decision can feel a bit like a revolution, and it is good to remember to have fun. As a leader of change, it is your duty. If there isn't some theater in what you are communicating, you are missing an opportunity. Turn the music up, drop confetti from the ceiling, hold the doors until the grand opening, and implement a bit of ceremony—whatever it takes to kick off the storytelling.

This fun can show up in how we name things. "The difference between Pepsi Max and Diet Pepsi, the difference between delicious, colorful vegetables and healthy vegetables, the difference between *frustration-free packaging* and *green packaging*" Sunstein explained, "are targeting some action or product and associating it with something in the vicinity, at least, of fun. That can be a great motivator of behavior change. When people think X is more fun than Y, the choice of X is starting to look better."

Think of the words you use in your story, the plotline of your communications, how you can demonstrate the decision or celebrate wins with flair, and make sure that you attract people to be a part of the change.

MAKE IT PERSONAL

The Roman emperor and stoic philosopher, Marcus Aurelius, wrote that "'o one objects to what is useful to him." If you find others objecting, it may be a sign that people don't find what you are telling them to be useful to them personally.

Martyn Etherington, who we met earlier, is the chief marketing officer at TeraData, a $1.8-billion-dollar data analytics company headquartered in San Diego, California. He was telling me about an article from *National Geographic* that influenced his thinking on change management.

"The author of the article was talking about high infant mortality rates in African villages due to poor water quality and cultural norms that prevented good infant care," he explained. A doctor went to the village and found what Etherington called "positive deviants." These were "women whom their communities admired. They might not have been the chief's wife or in a position of authority, but others would listen to them. They were looked up to," he explained. The doctor convinced these women to make the right medical choices and to tell others what they had learned. Using those positive deviants, they were able to change the medical outcomes and save lives. The information wasn't resisted because it was now seen as useful.

"I have since applied this to my work as a leader," he continued. "It might not be those in leadership positions that have the ear of the organization." In his current work, they are undergoing a transformation. To prepare, Etherington got leaders in a room and wrote on a whiteboard a list of employees who were the "go-to" people in France, Germany, Japan, China, the States, and all of their markets and functions.

"Sometimes it was a leader, but often it was a person lower in the organization that held influence," he said. In

San Francisco, it was the office manager who knew everyone and was very visible. Regardless of rank, they found those who could be brought into the story, trained, and equipped to help with the change. "We made them ambassadors, giving them information, early access to research, to content, and the new brand," all aimed at helping these change agents have influence. "This made all the difference," he concluded. "Some flat earthers came over to the cause. Others didn't make the transition. But in the end, we were able to affect change in the organization."

When considering a big change at LEARFIELD recently, I included a question in the employee survey which asked, "Who in the organization would you expect to have an opinion about this topic?" That question resulted in a list of influencers, at all levels and across all functions, that served as very useful sounding boards to the development of ideas and are poised to help with implementation. If you can influence people's thinking personally through relationships, it can be more successful.

MAKE IT A MECHANISM

In an Amazon employee all-hands meeting in February 2008, Jeff Bezos said that when there is a recurring problem in the organization, the temptation is to get the group together and ask them to *try harder* or *do better*. He claimed this rarely worked because when you ask for good intentions, you are not asking for change. Your team already had good intentions, at least we hope so. "Good intentions don't work, but mechanisms do," Bezos concluded.

The same is true not just for problem-solving but for any kind of change you wish to implement. No matter how much fun it is or how repetitive you are with your messaging, you can't just tell people to *change*. You have to put into practice the processes that convert inputs to outputs in a consistent way leveraging everything the organization can bring to bear—people, processes, technology, organization design, measurements, recognition, and reward systems. Only then is the change actionable and likely to stick. A mechanism is a set of inputs and feedback steps that create the outputs you want. Things like using premortems to de-risk decisions, implementing training, and monitoring anecdotes from the contact center for insights can all be mechanisms. They can be simple or complex, but any lasting change uses them. The design and implementation of mechanisms start with and is propelled by communication.

In 1983, Billy Joel released a song that hit the #1 Billboard Hot 100 charts entitled "Tell her About It." In the song, he urges his friend to tell the nice girl everything he feels and give her a reason to accept his sincerity. He continues doling out advice, offering that his friend should communicate constantly, give the girlfriend attention, and ultimately make her a believer. This is good advice, not only for the boy in the song who needs a little romantic encouragement, for every leader who wants to engender commitment.

PRO TIPS:
- Implement loudly to ensure everyone can see what the change means.
- Be vigilant about transparency. Things discussed behind closed doors should justify that confidentiality.
- Make the decision, and the implementation plans memorable by acting them out.
- Make them contagious by appealing to emotions and a common sense of urgency.

- Make the decision and resulting change memorable through repetition.
- Make it fun to be a part of the change.
- Look for influencers beyond the core team.
- Go beyond good intentions to make change actionable for the organization.

CHAPTER 14:

MAKING DECISIONS RIGHT

"Life is a matter of choices, and every choice you make makes you."

—JOHN C. MAXWELL, AUTHOR AND BUSINESS ADVISOR

Ann Sacks is an internationally known tile designer and entrepreneur. She sold the tile company she built to Kohler in 1989, and luxury tile showrooms all over the world still bear her name. Hers is a story of experimentation, taste making, and purposeful legacy.

"When I started the tile business, I found it comprehensively challenging," she recalled in a recent conversation. Without a background in the industry, "learning and making decisions is all I did," she recalled.

"I made uninformed decisions every day and every minute. I didn't know how to ship tile. I didn't know how to die cut. I didn't know what kinds of tiles were out there or what customers needed. These were unknowns." When she thinks back on those early days as a small business owner, her "biggest decision was just to continue."

As an entrepreneur, her problem-solving and creativity kept her innovating. "I was working with one of our suppliers and advised that they turn the tile over and glaze the back," Sacks recounted with a chuckle. "They were shocked and wondered why anyone would want a tile with rough edges. I told them I could charge three times as much for something with that unfinished look." Although skeptical, the partner trusted her after years of working together and made the samples. "Within a few months, five hotels specified that product, and we sold 300k square feet of it," she recalled.

"How did I know it would work?" she asked rhetorically. "I didn't. But I did know that tile from Morocco, which had a lot of imperfections, was a huge seller. It was also hugely expensive, impossible to get, and we had no control over color. I thought that I could get a similar look at a fraction of the price with none of the inherent problems. It was worth a try."

Sacks credits this sense of experimentation and imagination for her success, echoing the wisdom of two-way doors. "The best decision-making advice I have is to be willing to say, 'It's worth a try,'" she continued. "It's a simple comment, but behind it lies a deep understanding of what an experiment might mean to my partners and to me. If we were to try something, they would take on manufacturing risk. I was committing to market the product." There was an investment on both sides, but if you know the business and your customer, these are managed risks.

But was everything worth a try? No. She had her own version of a "not to do" list.

"What made the Ann Sacks brand was not only deciding what to carry, but what not to carry," she said. This kind of curation is often overlooked, especially when there is pressure to grow revenue or to meet competitive threats. "I got to the point where I could say 'this is not us.' We were known for the things we did well and known for what we didn't do," Sacks said. "You have to know what is important to you." What you want to be known for as a brand and as a leader?

At the time, many in the tile business assumed that products which were more decorated were more beautiful and more expensive. Sacks bucked the trends to differentiate. "I kept peeling back the industry to a greater level of simplicity." She couldn't hide in decoration, so she had to choose great materials and craftsmanship. Choice by choice, "the hallmark of the stores became this surprising simplicity," Sacks said. "Customers knew they were walking into a luxury retail environment to make a luxury purchase."

As the company grew, the choices were not just up to her, and she had the responsibility of making sure everyone understood the brand. "A disappointed salesperson would come to me and say that they lost an $87,000 order because we didn't carry a decorative trim that our competitors had," she recalled.

"I would use that opportunity to teach them about our business. I would tell them that in order to make the $87,000 sale, I would have to stock $250,000 of a trim tile that might not move and which our competitors carried. And if I invested in the inventory, I would need to allocate showroom space to it, and I wasn't crazy about how it would look in the store. It wasn't us."

"We became a strong brand because we made those choices. We became a brand because we made choices that were not just about design," Sacks added. "Anything that detracted from the model was filtered out, and what was left with pared-down and profitable." This was a far cry from when she first brought a shoebox of Mexican tile to a distributor in an early sales call and was told that it was just like all the product that they already could source. She learned her lesson. "In order to be successful, I had to think not only about what was beautiful, but what was missing that I could provide." Those early learnings helped define success.

The Ann Sacks brand, like all of our businesses, was built through hundreds of choices, layered like glaze on tile to create something that lasts.

MAKING DECISIONS RIGHT: START WITH MEASURING THE RIGHT THINGS

Melinda Sych told me recently how *not* to implement a successful transformation: try to solve everything perfectly at once. Sych, the vice president of global sales operations at Tektronix, has parlayed her technical experience across different roles and industries to help companies move from transactional product selling to solution selling and recurring revenue models.

"When driving transformative change, there are many decisions to make," she explained. "It's important to focus on the ones that are the highest priority first and then evaluate and make those changes in ways that allow your team to learn and evolve their approach versus trying to make every decision perfectly from the start." Installing hinges on decisions is critical for learning at pace. If you are not obsessed with short-term perfection, you can "move quickly and be more nimble," she advised.

She approaches these efforts by taking the time to understand the market dynamics and needs of the customer and what they value. "If you have not properly scoped and defined your focus, your team will lose traction or worse, they will develop a solution your customer does not want and will not use," she observed.

"You have to eat the elephant one bite at a time," Sych added. Whether it is a problem you have created for yourself or a problem that is driven by outside factors, prioritization is key. "I coach my teams to prioritize the problems to be solved, to be able to clearly articulate why that problem is their immediate focus, and then clearly identify the decisions they are making and the actions that are a result of those decisions to be made," she said. "This allows us to be very intentional when we make changes and to measure the impact those decisions have quickly and clearly." This is especially critical because the large-scale transformations, like the kind Sych has been a part of, require changes at a molecular level.

"We sometimes think because the decision can be made, a solution can be implemented, or the technology is possible that our people will immediately adjust and adopt our new way of doing business. But that is not always true," Sych observed. It requires a cultural change. Like Brent Michael from EverCommerce, Sych advises inviting employees and customers to come along on the journey.

To facilitate this work, Sych advises her teams to set aside ninety minutes a week to monitor the market. "They may talk to customers, they might talk to sellers, they might read industry forums or technology news," she explained. "This is time set aside to ensure they stay customer-focused and that their point of view is relevant with a world that does not stand still." This balance of day-to-day operations and market input keeps the long-term view in mind, even in times of transformation.

In cases where competition is steep, and customers are demanding, "timing is everything," Sych added. "You could have the perfect solution and be late, and you're done." The measure of a decision isn't just outcome, but the speed at which the outcomes were achieved and the risk that was assumed in the process.

"I use experimentation as a way to mitigate the risk of big investments," she continued. "I look for and teach my teams to create the lowest fidelity way to test something." Applying the concept of two-way doors, "if we are going to change the way we engage with a customer and we are going to use an automated tool to do it, we might start with a picture of a product on a piece of paper to test with a customer." It might take a long time to develop the real system, so creating a prototype can ensure that they are headed in the right direction.

Sych once launched a new solution in the semiconductor market while working for The Dow Chemical Company, which extended the up-time of the customer process by ten times but required significant process changes and a new selling model. Addressing an existing customer space, they "solved a pain point that our customer did not even realize that they had and positioned us as a market leader in a new space that we created," she said.

The key to success was presenting the return-on-investment data clearly so that customers could make decisions quickly. This holds lessons for all of us leading organizations through change initiatives. The reasons for action should be presented clearly, and the progress toward the goal tracked. Just like Sych and her team needed to convince customers that innovation was adding value, so you have to position change.

"If you wait for your customer to ask for the innovation, you are likely so far behind your competition that you are never going to win," Sych observed. "You have to be proactive and understand the job of the customer, and through listening, you can come up with a solution that changes things for the better." You have to understand why they are hiring your company and what skills you need to build to satisfy their needs. This is true when solving customer problems or implementing those solutions in your organization. Focusing on, measuring, and reporting the right things is a key part of storytelling on the way to transformation.

THE MAKING OF A HIGH-STAKES DECISION

In 2006, Trip Jobe was director of marketing for Neenah Paper, Inc, which had spun out of Kimberly-Clark a few years early. "At the time, we were number one or number two in our markets," he recalled in a recent conversation. "We were looking to grow and reinvest some proceeds from the sale of some paper pulp plants and timber assets." He dove into an analysis of the business by customer segment, charting the strengths and weaknesses in five categories.

"We were not ready to venture out of our core markets but saw some untapped adjacencies." They identified Fox River Paper Company, in Appleton, Wisconsin, as an acquisition target. Like is typical for these deals, the analysis was clear: combined, the brands would enjoy either the top or number two market positions in each of those five categories that Jobe identified.

Mergers and acquisitions are the quintessential high-stakes business decision fraught with risk. Yet, according to a 2018 survey by Deloitte, 79 percent of US corporations and private equity firms expect to see an increase in mergers and acquisitions. Since 2000, more than 790,000 transactions have been announced worldwide with a known value of over

$57 trillion, according to the Institute of Mergers, Acquisitions, and Alliances (IMAA).

Harvard Business Review identifies "lack of due diligence" and "miscalculating synergies" as key risk factors to making mergers and acquisitions fail. For this reason, the extensive analysis goes into making decisions of this impact. This was certainly true of Neenah.

Yet, as we know, results weren't going to come because of an Excel spreadsheet exercise done in the due diligence phase. In the end, "it would not have been successful if it hadn't been followed by countless other decisions considered holistically," Jobe recalled. "So much went into making this a success."

Jobe started the integration of the two companies with the customer-facing organizations. "We got the sales team aligned, and the brand strategy worked out to provide growth in the long-term." Then there were synergies and cost savings that were planned for operations. "We knew in the combination that we'd need to shut down some of the mills and plants. The whole industry had too many assets and as a market leader, this was true for us as well," he recalled.

In order to ensure the smooth shut down of those properties, they outlined a retention bonus strategy that would secure the talent they needed to finish strong. He recounted that these decisions were not without controversy.

When the executive team was reviewing that plan, one person noticed that there was a finance leader on the stay-on bonus list who had been at the company for less than fifteen months. "'Why would we offer a retention bonus to someone so new?' the leader asked. The general counsel replied, 'who in this room has been here less than two years?' and several hands were raised, including the acquisition leader and the associate general counsel. After a few 'touchés' and 'good points' were exchanged, the CEO reiterated that if the team thought someone needed a retention bonus, they would be eligible. If a different decision had been made that day on this one issue, we might have had losses in those plants or crises to navigate," Jobe surmised.

In the wake of the acquisition, the CEO and leadership team was adamant that every employee needed to be talked to about the announcement within a week of the acquisition, and within thirty days, everyone needed to know what their job would be with the new entity or what their severance plan entailed. "This commitment to communication from the top allowed us to make those hard decisions quickly and start moving forward," Jobe recalled.

"When we acquired the company, we had approximately ten brands under which we sold paper, and Fox River had about twenty-six, mostly attained through acquisitions," Jobe recalled. "We ended up whittling that down to fifteen." To inform these decisions, they studied the sales results, market positioning, product design, and cross-functional inter-dependencies. "If we decided to close down the one plant capable of making one grade or brand of paper, we had to figure out how to move the operations or what we could do differently."

Most decisions were straightforward. However, "About 25 percent of the decisions, affecting the 20 percent of our business, required the most research and consideration of alternatives," he said. "Some of the specialty products were valuable but did not enjoy volumes that would justify keeping a dedicated mill open to produce."

Here they remained stubborn on the goal but flexible on some of the details. At one point in the brand and factory con-solidation, Jobe went to a distributor saying they planned to reduce the number of color options in one category from six to two based on what was selling. The distributor explained that the extra colors were a differentiator in the market and had helped secure the office store printing shop business. "Based on that feedback, we kept the extra colors, took their suggestion of the brand name to keep, and enjoyed growth in that line for years to come," Jobe said. "Through these experiences, we learned that decisions should be vetted by customers before they were finalized." He summarized his experience by saying, "Listening is the first step to making great decisions."

Listening isn't enough. What you hear must be turned into action. Unlike goals which can be narrow in scope and binary in achievement (you either won the gold medal in the Olympics or you didn't; your business either topped the *Inc* Fastest Growing Companies list, or it didn't), systems are the processes or mechanisms by which you layer skills, gather insights, and communicate progress to achieve success.

This is exactly what Neenah Paper did when they used direct customer feedback to adjust their post-integration plans and make the business successful. It wasn't just the high-stakes decision by the CEO or a small team of leaders to acquire Fox River that leads to success. It was the hundreds of decisions afterward. Again, it is a myth, and a dangerous one at that, to believe that there is a solitary good or bad decision. It was everything that happened after the decision that truly *made* the decision right.

WELCOMING IN DECISIONS

"More and more, I feel like my job is decision making," said Kenji Kuramoto, founder of Acuity, a financial services firm headquartered in Atlanta, Georgia. I was speaking to him five days after they had announced the acquisition of Counting House Associates, a New Hampshire-based firm.

This acquisition aligns to the overall growth plan Kuramoto and his management team put in place, allowing the firm to grow to more than one hundred employees since first started in 2004.

The work to finalize the deal, which took months, was behind them, but now the work of integration was ahead. "The key to my being able to delegate decisions is having a strong management team," he said, echoing the earlier chapter on talent density. "We have team members, thank goodness, who are very excited to integrate this acquisition," he continued. Enthusiasm and expertise for the task helps teams with motivation.

As does a commitment to communication. There is nothing worse than leaving your people in the dark. Finding ways to communicate with the entire staff can be challenging, but in my experience, as in Kuramoto's, overthinking it can be a roadblock. He told me as they transitioned from a small organization to a much larger one through acquisitions and mergers, he had miscalculated how his communications were perceived; some of his leadership team understood the strategy, but the rest of the company did not.

In response, he implemented an OKR (objectives and key results) methodology on a ninety-day cycle of goal setting, which gave visibility across the organization. Further, he recorded weekly videos for employees in which he speaks about the goals, the progress, and about what is happening in the accounting sector. Kuramoto says he tries to keep it light and will sometimes "show up in a Halloween costume." This is all to connect the big ideas to the day-to-day work and have some fun. "I find that once people understand the thinking behind the decision, that makes all the difference. It gives us the best odds to implement well." Keeping the why in the forefront helps not only with making but implementing decisions.

With the acquisition tasks so fresh on his mind, he explained how this combination of communication, context, and goal-setting plays out. "One of my OKRs this quarter is about making the transition of the Counting House employees and clients smooth. Making them feel welcome. It isn't just about growth or revenue. It about growing our community now."

Using words of hospitality, Kuramoto describes how he thinks about integration. "Acquisitions provide our team with more opportunities to grow and to serve more clients. And it's not going to work unless we are welcoming. Unless we are bringing the new people over and they feel as proud to be a part of the company as we are to have them. The clients need to know we are excited," he added. Running a great business, he said, is "about marrying up inspiration with accountability."

The same can be true of decision making. Leaders and employees welcome decisions into the organization with the same thoughtful process, commitment to communication, customer insight, and thoughtful measurement and analysis. Kuramoto understands that the value of the acquisition won't come because management decided to sign the paperwork to transfer capital and employment contracts. Like all business decisions of note, the value will come in the host of follow-on choices that will be made by the organization in the future.

If you accept the notion that decisions are not solitary acts of inspiration but the starting line for a lot of work in our organizations, you can make decisions right. With the mindset and systems in place, you can ensure that your decisions are appropriate, considered, and most importantly, well-made.

ACKNOWLEDGMENTS

———

Thank you to everyone who made this book possible. So many showed their support of my journey as an author by backing the publication as patrons and by sharing out the news, liking my posts and updates, and encouraging me along the way.

Thank you to my pre-sales campaign supporters:

Alex Alderman

Rob Allen

Anthony Anticole

Luke Arehart

Andreina Bacigalupo

Kevin C. Barlow

Linda Bartley

Drew Battistelli

Jasper Bawcom

Angela Bennett-Glock

Daniel Bruton

Steve Bryan

Emily Buchenberger

Teresa Caro

David Carroll

Erica Carroll

Gabriel Carruana

Katie Cecil Hunt

Cortney Chalifoux

Nina Church-Adams

Susan K. Clark

Benjamin Clifton

Larry Coburn

Jill Cochran

Bruce Cook

Corrie Cook

Sandra Cummings

Leslie Curl

Jennifer Daniels

Sophia Danvers

Christine C Davis

Justin Davis

Tom Davis

Tony Davis

Jeff Day
Monique Devine
Sabrina DiCiano
Joseph R. Dickerson
Nicole Diltz
John Dixon
Tara Dowdell
Amanda Eberle Boyer
Lindsey Erlick
Romeo Estores
Angela L. Evans
Kristi Z. Flores
Bill Fons
Riana Frischman
Deonna Gandy
Alyssa Gasca
Gianna Gaudini
Jordan Gertzman
Jamin Gluck
Julie Golzarian
Patricia Gooden
Michelle Grabel-Komar
Lisa Graddy
Kathleen Grave
Randy Hai
Sarah Halstead
Jessica Handler
Heidi Haneberg
Karie Harris
Dan Hasker
Brooks Heiser
Irene Higgins

Becky Hoffman
Katherine Jacobs
Betsy Jaffe
Trip Jobe
Luke Jordan
Natan Klein
Eric Koester
Tim Lauer
Sheridan Lea
Ji Li
EJ Liao
Juan Luis Garcia
Ashley Lyon
Adrian Malatesta
Katie Mathews
Cary Mathews
Cheryl Mathews
Lindsey McCauley
Reilly McClure
Cindy McCullough
Norman Miglietta
Judith Miller
Joel Mitchell
Tracy Moore
John Morton
Rob Morton
Ross Mullins
Nader Nanjiani
Drew Neisser
Matt Neylon
Karen Nishikawa
Kristen O'Connor

William Paredes
Gerry Perkel
Jennifer Perrella
Samantha Phenix
Tina Pierce
Julie Pond
Sussy Portillo
Vijay Rao
Ryan Reichert
Shane Riddle
Gina Riley
Tina Rust
Jessica Sadler
Steve Seminario
Beth Shepherd
Gaylyn Sher-Jan
Jeffery Shumate
Bailey Smith
Kirk Strobeck
Joshua Stump

Tristan Tanovan-Fox
Kami Toufar
Le Tran
Tim Turner
Angelica Turner
Vijita U. G.
Susan Velasco
Jamie Voisin
Rebecca Walters
Lynette and James Walters
David Walters
Ed Watson
Kim Way
Kristi White
Melanie Winters-Blodgett
Roneisha Worthy
Ozlem Yilmaz
Tanya Young Stump
Bob Yund
Gloria Zabel

This group represents friends and colleagues, new and old, who have poured into me their expertise, advice, energy, and support. Many on this list I credit directly for the lessons of this book and the success I have had in my career.

Special thanks to all my beta readers Marcia Blenko, Teresa Caro, Leslie Curl, Claire Davis, Tony Davis, Jerry Dawson, Sue Dawson, Alyssa Gasca, Roger Gardner, Patricia Gooden, Randy Hain, Helene Lollis, Tracy Moore, Erick Petersen, Samantha Phenix, Dann Pierce, Sean Riley, and Allan White. Whether they read a chapter or two or the whole book, I am appreciative of the insights and perspective they offered. The book you now hold would not have been possible without their partnership and each had an impact.

Thank you to Morgan Wider and Melissa Proctor for inspiring me with your own author journeys. To Eric Koester, the team at Georgetown University and the Creator Institute, and crack team at New Degree Press, including my editors Al Bagdonas and Vivian Rose Cummings, my copy editor Leah Pickett, and my layout editor Ruslan Nabiev. Your patience, skill, and expertise made this book better! Thank you to Bailey Smith, whose practical support helped me in more ways than you know. Thank you to Gjorji Pejkovski, Dania Z., and Rebecca Walters for the cover art design and consultation.

And finally, I want to thank my family, without whom this book would not have been possible. They put up with my late nights, distracting weekends, and deadline stress, showing unwavering support. They encouraged me in the task, celebrated my small victories, and should in every way consider this their book. I appreciate my parents, who have always been my biggest cheerleaders. Doug and Claire, my awesome kids, for giving me the space to write, believing in me, and inspiring me every day. And to my husband and best friend, Tony. Marrying you is the best decision I have ever made!

APPENDIX

———

INTRODUCTION

Edison, Thomas. Quoted in the *Harper's Monthly* Magazine, September 1932.

Martin, Roger L. "M&A: The One Thing You Need to Get Right." *Harvard Business Review,* June 2016.

"Q&A with Kevin Sharkey" *Ideas of Order*. Volume 3. Published September 25, 2019. Accessed June 12, 2021. https://issuu.com/californiaclosets/docs/ioo_vol3_digitalissue_final.

CHAPTER 1

"Annual Report Statistics." Delaware Division of Corporations. https://corp.delaware.gov/stats/, accessed June 12, 2021.

Bezos, Jeff. "Letter to Shareholders" *1997 Amazon Annual Report*. Published March 30, 1998. Accessed June 12, 2021. https://s2.q4cdn.com/299287126/files/doc_financials/annual/Shareholderletter97.pdf.

Blank, Steven. *The Four Steps to the Epiphany*. Louisville, Kentucky: cafepress.com, 2006.

Chopra, Deepak. *The Book of Secrets*. New York: Harmony, 2005.

Eng, Dinah. "Nick Swinmurn: Zappos' silent founder." *Fortune,* September 5, 2012. https://fortune.com/2012/09/05/nick-swinmurn-zappos-silent-founder/.

Fosco, Molly. "World's Biggest Corporate Tax Haven? It's No Paradise Island." *OZY* September 2, 2018. Accessed June 12, 2021, https://www.ozy.com/around-the-world/worlds-biggest-corporate-tax-haven-its-no-paradise-island/87954/.

Garvin, David A. and Michael Roberto. "What You Don't Know About Making Decisions." *Harvard Business Review,* September 2001. https://hbr.org/2001/09/what-you-dont-know-about-making-decisions.

Hamilton, Walter. "KKR buying CarsDirect.com owner Internet Brands for $1.1 billion." *Los Angeles Times,* June 3, 2014. https://www.latimes.com/business/la-fi-kkr-internet-brands-20140604-story.html.

Herman, Lily. "37 Inspiring Quotes from Expert Women in Tech." *Skillcrush*. https://skillcrush.com/blog/advice-from-women-in-tech/.

KPMG. "Cayman Islands—Overview and Introduction." November 1, 2019. Accessed June 12, 2021, https://home.kpmg/xx/en/home/insights/2011/12/cayman-islands-overview-introduction.html.

La Duke, Phil. "Moira Vetter: 'Make Mistakes faster and move on'." *ThriveGlobal,* November 19, 2020. https://thriveglobal.com/stories/moira-vetter-make-mistakes-faster-and-move-on/.

"Lessons Learned from Bill Gross' 35 IPOs/Exits and 40 Failures." *First Round Review*. Accessed June 12, 2021, https://firstround.com/review/Lessons-Learned-from-Bill-Gross-35-IPOs-and-40-Failures/.

Lovdahl Gormsen, Liz. "How the European commission Lost Its Tax Battle Against Ireland and Apple." *Promarket, the publication of the Stigler Center at the University of Chicago Booth School of Business.* August 28, 2020. Accessed June 12, 2021, https://promarket.org/2020/08/18/how-the-european-commission-lost-its-tax-battle-against-ireland-and-apple/.

Nelson, Nick Brandpreneur Brand Tribe *Instagram*. January 22, 2021. Accessed June 12, 2021, https://www.instagram.com/p/CKWa2_Ghgql/.

Ries, Eric. *The Lean Startup.* New York: Crown Business, 2011.

Reuters Staff. "KKR to buy Internet Brands for $1.1 billion." June 3, 2014. Accessed June 12, 2021. https://www.reuters.com/article/us-internetbrands-deals-kkr/kkr-to-buy-internet-brands-for-1-1-billion-idUSKBN0EE12V20140603.

Rutt, John Towill. *Life and Correspondence of Joseph Priestley in Two Volumes.* 1831. Accessed June 12, 2021. https://books.google.com/books?.id=psMGAAAAQAAJ&pg=PR7&source=gbs_selected_pages&cad=3#v=onepage&q&f=false. See entry for September 10, 1772, on page 182.

Sollisch, Jim. "The Cure of Decision Fatigue." *Wall Street Journal,* June 10, 2016. https://www.wsj.com/articles/the-cure-for-decision-fatigue-1465596928.

Vetter, Moira. *AdVenture: An Outside's Inside View of Getting an Entrepreneur to Market.* Noyo Press: 2013.

"What Difference Do Women Entrepreneurs Make Anyway?" Frazier & Deeter Blog. Accessed June 12, 2021, https://www.frazierdeeter.com/articles/what-difference-do-women-entrepreneurs-make-anyway/.

CHAPTER 2

Alofs, Paul. "A Leaders' most important decision: hiring." *The Globe and Mail,* March 20, 2017. Accessed June 12, 2021, https://www.theglobeandmail.com/report-on-business/careers/leadership-lab/a-leaders-most-important-decision-hiring/article34346310/.

Blank, Arthur. *Good Company.* New York: Harper Collins, 2020.

Catmull, Ed. *Creativity, Inc.* New York: Random House, 2014.

"CEO Jeff Weiner to move into Executive Chairman role and Ryan Roslansky, Senior Vice President of Product, to become CEO on June 1." *LinkedIn Press Room.* February 5, 2020. Accessed June 12, 2021. https://news.linkedin.com/2020/february/linkedin-ceo-jeff-weiner-to-move-into-executive-chairman-role-an.

Cooper, Kindra. "Decoding the Interview process at Microsoft." *Candor,* July 13, 2020. Accessed June 12, 2021, https://candor.co/articles/interview-prep/decoding-the-interview-process-at-microsoft-interview

Eno, Brian. *A Year with Swollen Appendices.* New York: Faber and Faber, 1996.

Felps, Will, Terence R. Mitchell, and Eliza Byington. "How, When, and Why Bad Apple Spoil the Barrel: Negative Group Members and Dysfunctional Groups." *Research in Organizational Behavior.* Volume 27, 2006. Accessed June 12, 2021, https://s3-us-west-2.amazonaws.com/oww-files-public/a/a5/Final_BA_ROB.pdf.

Groth, Aimee. "You're The Average Of The Five People You Spend The Most Time With." *Business Insider,* July 24, 2012. Accessed June 21, 2021, https://www.businessinsider.com/jim-rohn-youre-the-average-of-the-five-people-you-spend-the-most-time-with-2012-7.

Hastings, Reed and Erin Meyer. *No Rules Rules: Netflix and the Culture of Reinvention.* New York: Penguin Press, 2020.

"Individual Productivity Variation in Software Development." Construx. Accessed June 21, 2021, https://www.construx.com/blog/productivity-variations-among-software-developers-and-teams-the-origin-of-10x/

Kleon, Austin. *Show Your Work!* New York: Workman Publishing, 2014.

Kuittinen, Tero. "Nokia's destiny: from boots to phones to… boots." BGR, July 1, 2014. Accessed June 12, 2021, https://bgr.com/2014/07/01/nokia-future-analysis-smart-shoes/.

"Raising the Bar—The Unconventional Interview Method That Really Works." *SocialTalent.* Accessed June 12, 2021, https://www.socialtalent.com/blog/recruitment/raising-the-bar-unconventional-interview-method-really-works.

Sackman, Harold, W.J. Erikson, and E.E. Grant. "Exploratory experimental studies comparing online and offline programming performance." *Communications of the ACM,* January 1968. Accessed June 21, 2021, https://dl.acm.org/doi/10.1145/362851.362858.

Seidman, David. "What is the Microsoft Hiring Process Like and What Really Happens Behind the Scenes After an Interview." *Quora.* Accessed June 12, 2021, https://www.quora.com/What-is-the-Microsoft-hiring-process-like-and-what-really-happens-behind-the-scenes-after-an-interview.

"The Real cost of bad hiring decisions." *Sonru Blog.* February 1, 2016. Accessed January 15, 2021, https://www.sonru.com/blog/the-real-cost-of-bad-hiring-decisions/.

Wiener, Jeff. "The Most Valuable Lesson I've Learned as a CEO." *LinkedIn Pulse,* February 3, 2014. Accessed June 12, 2021, https://www.linkedin.com/pulse/20140203145935-22330283-the-most-valuable-lesson-i-ve-learned-as-a-ceo/.

CHAPTER 3

Acar, Oguz A., Murat Tarakci, and Daan van Knippenberg. "Why Constraints Are Good for Innovation." *Harvard Business Review,* November 22, 2019. https://hbr.org/2019/11/why-constraints-are-good-for-innovation

Ariely, Dan. *Predictably Irrational.* New York: Harper Perennial, 2008.

Gery, Zac. "Searching for Nails: A Hammer's Story." *Code Project.* October 31, 2013. Accessed June 12, 2021, https://www.codeproject.com/Articles/677006/Searching-For-Nails-A-Hammers-Story.

Goldsmith, Marshall. *What Got You Here Won't Get You There.* New York: Hachette Books, 2007.

Herman, Lily. "37 Inspiring Quotes from Expert Women in Tech." *Skillcrush.* Accessed on June 12, 2021, https://skillcrush.com/blog/advice-from-women-in-tech/.

Juneja, Prachi. "How to Develop a Long Term Perspective." *Man-*

agement Study Guide. Accessed June 12, 2021, https://www.man-agementstudyguide.com/how-to-develop-long-term-perspec-tive.htm.

Purton, Leon. "The First Three Things you need to do when you get Promoted to Leadership." *Medium,* October 19, 2019. Accessed June 12, 2021, https://medium.com/sparks-publication/the-first-three-things-you-need-to-do-when-you-get-promoted-to-lead-ership-d6360687ab00.

Malone, Thomas W., Robert Laubacher, and Tammy Johns. "The Big Idea: The Age of Hyperspecialization." *Harvard Business Review,* July-August 2011.

Maslow, Abraham. *Psychology of Science: A Reconnaissance*. New York: HarperCollins, 1966.

Molosi, Hugh. "Falling in Love with the Problem, Part 1." *Lean Start-up Co. Education Program Blog.* Accessed June 12, 2021, https://leanstartup.co/falling-love-problem/.

Rogers, Bruce. "Why 84% of Companies Fail at Digital Transfor-mation." *Forbes,* January 7, 2016. https://www.forbes.com/sites/brucerogers/2016/01/07/why-84-of-companies-fail-at-digital-trans-formation/?sh=7d3215c8397b.

Rogers, Paul and Marcia Blenko. "Who has the D?" *Harvard Business Review,* January 2006. https://hbr.org/2006/01/who-has-the-d-how-clear-decision-roles-enhance-organizatio-nal-performance

Thaler, Richard. *Misbehaving.* New York: W. W. Norton and Com-pany, 2015.

Warner Pacific University. *Experience Magazine,* Winter 2019. Jan-uary 5, 2020.

CHAPTER 4

Angelou, Maya. *Twitter.* September 2, 2018. Accessed June 12, 2021, https://twitter.com/DrMayaAngelou/status/1036327789488734208.

Austen, Ian. "Kodak Selling X-Ray and Medical Image Lines." *The New York Times,* January 11, 2007. https://www.nytimes.com/2007/01/11/business/11kodak.html.

Bezos, Jeff. *Invent & Wander.* Boston: Harvard Business Review Press, 2021.

Blank, Steven Gary. *The Four Steps to the Epiphany.* Louisville, Kentucky: Cafepress.com, 2006.

"Blue Ocean Strategic Moves." *Blue Ocean Strategy website.* Accessed June 12, 2021, https://www.blueoceanstrategy.com/bos-moves/cirque-du-soleil/

Christensen, Clayton M, Taddy Hall, Karen Dillon, and David S. Duncan. *Competing Against Luck,* New York: Harper Business, an imprint of HarperCollins, 2016.

Gorbman, Randy. "Kodak signs deals to continue supply of motion picture film." *WXXI News.* January 31, 2020. Accessed June 12, 2021, https://www.wxxinews.org/post/kodak-signs-deals-continue-supply-motion-picture-film.

"Health Imaging History." *Kodak Health Imaging website.* Accessed June 12, 2021, https://www.kodak.com/en/company/page/health-imaging-history.

Ingwer, Mark. *Empathetic Marketing.* London, England: Palgrave Macmillan, 2012.

Kim, W. Chan and Renée Mauborgne. *Blue Ocean Strategy.* Boston: Harvard Business School Press, 2005.

Levy, Steven. "Jack Dorsey created Twitter, now he's taking on the banks with Square." *Wired,* July 2, 2012. https://www.wired.co.uk/article/jack-dorsey.

"Meet Cheri Mims of Lilybelle Flowers, the Square Seller Who Rang the Bell." *SquareUp blog.* November 20, 2015. Accessed June 12, 2021, https://squareup.com/us/en/townsquare/meet-cheri-mims-of-lilybelle-flowers-the-square-seller-who-rang-the-bell.

"Milestones." *Kodak website.* Accessed June 12, 2021, https://www.kodak.com/en/company/page/milestones.

Miller, Donald. *Building A Story Brand.* New York: HarperCollins, 2017.

Penney, J.C. *Fifty Years with the Golden Rule: a spiritual autobiography.* New York: Harper & Brothers Publishing, 1950.

"Planar Announces Sale of Electroluminescent (EL) Business to Beneq." Accessed June 12, 2021, https://www.businesswire.com/news/home/20121130005314/en/Planar-Announces-Sale-of-Electroluminescent-EL-Business-to-Beneq.

Reicheld, Fred. "Prescription for Cutting Costs." Bain & Company. Accessed June 12, 2021, https://media.bain.com/Images/BB_Prescription_cutting_costs.pdf.

Salter, Chuck. "Most Innovative Companies: 2009: Amazon #9." *Fast Company,* February 10, 2009. Accessed June 12, 2021, https://www.fastcompany.com/company/amazon.

CHAPTER 5

Adelman, Jopseh M. "Did Hamilton Write Too Much for His Own Good?" *Early Americanist,* October 24, 2017. Accessed June 12, 2021, https://earlyamericanists.com/2017/10/24/did-hamilton-write-too-much-for-his-own-good/.

BayLive Media. "Pinterest CEO, Ben Silbermann, speaking at Startup Grind." *YouTube.* March 2, 2012. Accessed June 12, 2021, https://www.youtube.com/watch?v=1JLc2PYyCao.

Bezos, Jeff. Interview by Charlie Rose. June 28, 2000. https://charlierose.com/videos/17540.

"Runco Acquired by Planar." *Residential Systems.* May 23, 2007. Accessed June 12, 2021, https://www.residentialsystems.com/news/runco-acquired-by-planar.

Christensen, Clayton. "Jobs to Be Done." *Christensen Institute blog.* Accessed June 12, 2021, https://www.christenseninstitute.org/jobs-to-be-done/.

Clifford, Catherine. "How Mark Zuckerberg came up with the idea for Facebook." *CNBC Make It,* January 18, 2018. Accessed June 12, 2021, https://www.cnbc.com/2018/01/17/why-mark-zuckerberg-started-facebook.html

Davis, Jennifer. "Knowing What you Are About." *Jennifer Davis Blog.* June 2006. Accessed June 12, 2021, http://jenniferbdavis.blogspot.com/2006/06/knowing-what-you-are-about.html.

Drawbaugh, Ben. "Runco's first 3Dimesnion projector uses passive glasses." *Engadget.* September 23, 2010. Accessed June 12, 2021, https://www.engadget.com/2010-09-23-runcos-first-3dimension-projector-with-passive-glasses.html.

Graham, Jefferson. "The House that Helped Build Google." *USA Today,* July 4, 2007. Accessed June 12, 2021, https://usatoday30.usatoday.com/tech/techinvestor/corporatenews/2007-07-04-google-wojcicki_N.htm.

Ha, Anthony. "Daily Crunch: Calendly valued at $3B." *TechCrunch,* January 26, 2021. Accessed June 12, 2021, https://techcrunch.com/2021/01/26/daily-crunch-calendly-valued-at-3b/.

"High-End Projection Brand Runco Fades Away." *Sound & Vision,* March 8, 2016. Accessed June 12, 2021, https://www.soundandvision.com/content/high-end-projection-brand-runco-fades-away.

Howard, Caroline. "Google's Susan Wojcicki Takes Lead of Ads and Engineering." *Forbes,* May 6, 2011. https://www.forbes.com/sites/carolinehoward/2011/05/06/googles-susan-wojcicki-suddenly-lead-of-engineering-and-ads-she-wants-to-talk-about-chickens/?sh=58f7440179ea.

Kestenbaum, Richard. "Rent The Runway's Outsized $1 Billion Valuation Is Reportedly Coming Down To Earth." Forbes, May 27, 2020. Accessed June 12, 2021, https://www.forbes.com/sites/richardkestenbaum/2020/05/27/rent-the-runways-outsized-1-billion-valuation-is-reportedly-coming-down-to-earth/.

Kiam, Victor. "I liked the shaver so much I bought the company—

Remington ad from 1979." July 17, 2015. Video, 0:17. https://www.
youtube.com/watch?v=qf22bddvLnc.

"Pinterest Statistics for Business." HootSuite Blog. Accessed June 12,
2021, https://blog.hootsuite.com/pinterest-statistics-for-business/.

"Press." *Pinterest website.* Accessed June 12, 2021, https://about.pin-
terest.com/en/node/19/mailto%3Apress%40pinterest.com.

"Process." *Rent the Runway Website.* Accessed June 12, 2021, https://
www.renttherunway.com/about-us/process.

"Prophet Brand Relevance Index." Prophet. Accessed June 12, 2021,
https://www.prophet.com/relevantbrands-2019/.

Sims, Peter. *Little Bets: How Breakthrough Ideas Emerge from Small
Discoveries.* New York: Free Press, 2011.

"Story." *Rent the Runway Website.* Accessed June 12, 2021, https://
www.renttherunway.com/about-us/story

"The Holiday-You're supposed to be the leading lady of your own
life." November 30, 2015. Video. 1:11. https://www.youtube.com/
watch?v=9YSuVITrKqs.

"Victor Kiam Obituary." *The Telegraph.* May 30, 2001. Accessed
June 12, 2021, https://www.telegraph.co.uk/news/obituaries/1332089/
Victor-Kiam.html.

CHAPTER 6

Carter, Alexandra. *Ask for More.* New York: Simon & Schuster, 2020.

DMR Business Statistics. "25 Evernote Statistics and Facts (2020) |
By the Numbers." July 1, 2020. Accessed June 12, 2021, https://ex-
pandedramblings.com/index.php/evernote-statistics/.

Hammes, T.X. "Essay: Dumb-dumb bullets." *Armed Forces Journal,* July 1, 2009. Accessed June 12, 2021, http://armedforcesjour-
nal.com/essay-dumb-dumb-bullets/.

James, Geoffrey James. "Elon Musk and Jeff Bezos Banned PowerPoint. Here's Why" *Inc.com.* June 25, 2020.

Kellogg, Ronald T. *The Psychology of Writing*. Oxford: Oxford University Press, 1999.

"Kettering, Charles F." GM Heritage Center. Accessed June 12, 2021, https://web.archive.org/web/20130905025939/http://history.gmheritagecenter.com/wiki/index.php/Kettering,_Charles_F.

Lewis, C.S. "You Can Make Anything By Writing." Abbott Press Blog. Accessed June 12, 2021, https://blog.abbottpress.com/you-can-make-anything-by-writing/.

Lovallo, Dan and Olivier Sibony. "The Case for Behavioral Strategy." *McKinsey Quarterly*, March 1, 2010. Accessed June 12, 2021, https://www.mckinsey.com/business-functions/strategy-and-corporate-finance/our-insights/the-case-for-behavioral-strategy.

Merrill, Jacqueline Pfeffer. "Jeff Bezos' PowerPoint prohibition." *Philanthropy Daily*, August 9, 2013. https://www.philanthropydaily.com/jeff-bezos-powerpoint-prohibition/.

Parrish, Shane. Twitter. November 24, 2018. Accessed June 12, 2021, https://twitter.com/shaneaparrish/status/1066351268459819010.

Pascal, Blaise. *Les Provinciales*, or, *The Mystery of Jesuitisme*. London: Richard Royston, 1658. https://books.google.com/books?id=hEVPAQAAIAAJ&q=shorter&hl=en#v=snippet&q=shorter&f=false.

Williams, Margary. *Velveteen Rabbit*. New York: Doubleday, 1922.

Wiens, Kyle. "Your Company is Only As Good as Your Writing." *Harvard Business Review*, July 30, 2013. Accessed June 12, 2021, https://hbr.org/2013/07/your-company-is-only-as-good-a.

Wiens, Kyle and Julia Bluff. *Tech Writing Handbook*. Accessed June 12, 2021, https://help.dozuki.com/Tech_Writing.

CHAPTER 7

Ariely, Dan. *Predictably Irrational*. New York: Harper Perennial, 2008.

AT&T Wireless. "AT&T Wireless TV Commercial, 'Lily Uncomplicates: Buzzer Beaters.'" *iSpot.TV.* Accessed on June 13, 2021, https://www.ispot.tv/ad/OoFy/at-and-t-wireless-lily-uncomplicates-buzzer-beaters

AWS. "How Live Nation Realized Business Value with AWS." Executive Insights. Accessed June 12, 2021, https://aws.amazon.com/executive-insights/content/how-live-nation-realized-business-value-with-aws/.

Brookes, Joseph. "AWS CEO Andy Jassy's Four Elements of Transformation." *Which-50,* December 4, 2019. Accessed June 12, 2021, https://which-50.com/aws-ceo-andy-jassys-four-elements-of-transformation/.

Chernov, Bobby. "What percentage of start-ups fail?" *Review42,* November 21, 2020. Accessed June 12, 2021, https://review42.com/what-percentage-of-startups-fail/.

"Decision Making in the Age of Urgency." McKinsey & Company Survey. April 30, 2019. Accessed June 12, 2021, https://www.mckinsey.com/business-functions/organization/our-insights/decision-making-in-the-age-of-urgency.

Furrier, John. "Exclusive with Amazon's Cloud Chief: Enterprises must use cloud to transform." *Silicon Angle,* December 2, 2019. Accessed June 12, 2021, https://siliconangle.com/2019/12/02/exclusive-amazons-cloud-chief-enterprises-must-use-cloud-transform/.

Gaddis, Gay. *Cowgirl Power: how to kick-ass in business and life.* New York: Central Street, a Hachette Book Group, 2018.

McGrath, Jim. *The Little Book of Big Decision Models.* New York: FT Press, 2015.

"Introducing the Eisenhower Matrix." Eisenhower.me Website. Accessed June 12, 2021, https://www.eisenhower.me/eisenhower-matrix/.

Mankins, Michael C. and Richard Steele. "Stop Making Plans; Start Making Decisions." *Harvard Business Review,* January 2006. Accessed June 12, 2021, https://hbr.org/2006/01/stop-making-plans-start-making-decisions.

Patton, George. GeneralPatton.com website. Accessed June 12, 2021, https://www.generalpatton.com/quotes/.

TED. "Tim Urban: Inside the Mind of a Procrastinator." February 2016. Accessed June 12, 2021, https://www.ted.com/talks/tim_urban_inside_the_mind_of_a_master_procrastinator.

"The Consequences Model by Kristian Kreiner and Søren Christensen" Sketchbook Strategy. Accessed June 13, 2021, https://sketchbookstrategy.com/blog/2019/6/18/consequences-model.

"Turning Great Strategy into Great Performance." *Marakon Associates.* Accessed June 13, 2021, https://www.marakon.com/insights/hbr-turning-great-strategy-into-great-performance/.

Uglesbee, Ben. "3 retail turnaround success stories, and 3 turnarounds to watch." RetailDive, November 18, 2019. Accessed June 12, 2021, https://www.retaildive.com/news/3-retail-turnaround-success-stories-and-3-turnarounds-to-watch/567162/.

"We Are Live Nation." Live Nation Website. Accessed June 12, 2021, https://www.livenationentertainment.com/.

CHAPTER 8

Bariso, Justin. "The 5 Brilliant Emotional Intelligence Tactics this FBI Agent Uses to Negotiate." *Inc.,* May 26, 2016. Accessed June 12, 2021, https://www.inc.com/justin-bariso/how-an-fbi-agent-uses-emotional-intelligence-to-negotiate.html

Blakely, Sara. *Twitter.* December 21, 2020. Accessed June 12, 2021, https://twitter.com/SPANX/status/1341035767909519361

Carter, Alexandra. *Ask for More.* New York: Simon & Schuster, 2020.

Chugh, Dolly. *The Person You Mean To Be.* New York: Harper Collins, 2018.

Gaines, Chip. *Capital Gaines.* Nashville: W Publishing, 2017.

Hamilton, Isobel Asher. "Jeff Bezos Explains Why His Best Decisions Were Based Off Intuition, Not Analysis." *Business Insid-*

er, September 14, 2018. Accessed June 12, 2021, https://www.inc.com/business-insider/amazon-ceo-jeff-bezos-says-his-best-decision-were-made-when-he-followed-his-gut.html.

Heath, Chip and Dan Heath. *Decisive.* New York: Crown Publishing, 2013.

Kase, Larina. "Great Leaders are Great Decision-Makers." *Graziadio Business Review,* Pepperdine University. October 2010. Accessed June 12, 2021, https://gbr.pepperdine.edu/2010/10/great-leaders-are-great-decision-makers/.

Keeney, Ralph. "Personal Decisions Are the Leading Cause of Death." *Operation Research,* Volume 56, Issue 6. December 1, 2008. Accessed June 12, 2021, https://pubsonline.informs.org/doi/abs/10.1287/opre.1080.0588.

Kile, Meredith B. "'The Voice' Season 19 Premiere: John Legend Slams Blake Shelton in Hilarious Political Ad." *Entertainment Tonight.* October 19, 2020. Accessed June 12, 2021, https://www.etonline.com/the-voice-season-19-premiere-john-legend-slams-blake-shelton-in-hilarious-political-ad-155005.

Lamm, Greg. "With Washington Post, Jeff Bezos sees value in media's watchdog role." *Puget Sound Business Journal,* June 2016. Accessed June 12, 2021, https://www.bizjournals.com/seattle/blog/techflash/2016/06/with-washington-post-jeff-bezos-sees-value-in.html.

Markway, Barbara. "Why Self-Confidence is More Important Than You Think." Psychology Today, September 20, 2018. Accessed June 12, 2021, https://www.psychologytoday.com/us/blog/shyness-is-nice/201809/why-self-confidence-is-more-important-you-think.

Patterson, Kelsey. "HGTV Almost Axed 'Fixer Upper', but This Clip Saved the Show." *Popculture,* March 8, 2018. Accessed June 12, 2021, https://popculture.com/reality-tv/news/fixer-upper-chip-gaines-joanna-gaines-clip-saved-show/.

TEDGlobal. "Amy Cuddy: Your Body Language May Shape Who You Are." 2012. Accessed June 12, 2021, https://www.ted.com/talks/amy_cuddy_your_body_language_may_shape_who_you_are.

TEDxNorrkoping. "Dweck, Carol: The Power of Believing That You Can Improve." November 2014. Accessed June 12, 2021,https://www.ted.com/talks/carol_dweck_the_power_of_believing_that_you_can_improve.

Thaler, Richard. *Misbehaving.* New York: W. W. Norton & Company, 2015.

"The Last Word." *Bleecker Street Media.* Accessed June 12, 2021, https://bleeckerstreetmedia.com/thelastword

Thompson, Cadie. "Elon Musk: Model 3 production problems stem from Tesla getting 'overconfident' and 'too comfortable'." *Business Insider,* Feb 8, 2018. Accessed June 12, 2021, https://www.businessinsider.com/elon-musk-tesla-model-3-production-problems-causes-overconfident-batteries-2018-2.

Wanger, I. "Tesla—Statistics and Facts" *Statista* Feb 2, 2021.

CHAPTER 9

Bartz, Bianca. "A Look Inside Shopify's Culture with Daniel Weinand." *Hazel Blog.* March 9, 2017. Accessed June 12, 2021, https://hazelhq.com/blog/daniel-weinand-shopify-interview/.

Bell, Jennie. "Exclusive: Zappos is Looking Beyond e-commerce to ensure it lasts for 1,000 years." *Footwear News.* May 6, 2019

Bezos, Jeff. "2018 Letter to Shareholders." *Amazon website.* April 11, 2019. Accessed June 12, 2021, https://www.aboutamazon.com/news/company-news/2018-letter-to-shareholders.

Chamberlain, Andrew and Daniel Zhao. "The Key to Happy Customers? Happy Employees." *Harvard Business Review,* August 19, 2019. Accessed June 12, 2021, https://hbr.org/2019/08/the-key-to-happy-customers-happy-employees.

CNBC Television. "Airbnb co-founder and CEO Brian Chesky on starting the company." December 10, 2020. Video. https://www.youtube.com/watch?v=wTNfM1meJ9k.

Dickson, George. "Shopify's Brittany Forsyth on Scaling Company Culture." *Bonusly blog.* April 13, 2015 updated on July 11, 2019. Accessed on June 12, 2021, https://blog.bonus.ly/shopifys-brittany-forsyth-on-scaling-culture/.

Griffith, Erin. "Airbnb prices I.P.O. at $68 a share, for a $47 billion valuation." *The New York Times,* December 9, 2020. Accessed June 12, 2021, https://www.nytimes.com/2020/12/09/business/airbnb-ipo-price.html.

Heathfield, Susan M. "Find out how Zappos Reinforces its company culture." *The Balance Careers.* July 30, 2019. Accessed June 12, 2021, https://www.thebalancecareers.com/zappos-company-culture-1918813.

Hemerling, Jim, Julie Kilmann, Martin Daneosastro, Liza Stutts, and Cailin Ahern. "It's Not a Digital Transformation Without a Digital Culture." *Boston Consulting Group (BCG).* April 13, 2018. Accessed June 12, 2021, https://www.bcg.com/en-us/publications/2018/not-digital-transformation-without-digital-culture.

"How Happy Employees Lead to Happy Customers." Glassdoor blog. Published August 7, 2019. Accessed July 13, 2021, https://www.glassdoor.com/blog/glassdoor-reviews-customer-satisfaction.

Hsieh, Tony. *Delivering Happiness.* New York: Grand Central Publishing, 2013.

Hsieh, Tony. "Why I Sold Zappos." *Inc.* July 1, 2010. Accessed June 12, 2021, https://www.inc.com/magazine/20100601/why-i-sold-zappos.html.

Petrusewicz, Mary. "Professor draws on Intel for lessons on how big corporations succeed." *Stanford Report.* July 23, 2002. Accessed June 12, 2021, https://news.stanford.edu/news/2002/july24/burgelman-724.html.

"Planar Announces Industry's First Video Wall Designed Specifically for High-Traffic Public Spaces." *Benzinga.* November 30, 2010. Accessed on June 12, 2021, https://www.benzinga.com/press-releases/10/11/b652351/planar-announces-industrys-first-video-wall-designed-specifically-for-h

"Planar announces launch of Clarity Matrix LCD video wall." *Digital Signage Today,* June 1, 2009. Accessed June 12, 2021, https://www.digitalsignagetoday.com/news/planar-announces-launch-of-clarity-matrix-lcd-video-wall/.

Rapp, Jason. Twitter. November 28, 2020. Accessed June 12, 2021. https://twitter.com/jasonrapp/status/1332567061562736641.

Schultz, Howard. *Onward: How Starbucks Fought For Its Life Without Losing Its Soul.* New York: Rodale Press, 2012.

Taylor, Bill. "How One Fast-Food Chain Keeps Its Turnover Rates Absurdly Low." *Harvard Business Review,* January 26, 2016. Accessed June 12, 2021, https://hbr.org/2016/01/how-one-fast-food-chain-keeps-its-turnover-rates-absurdly-low.

"What's Wrong with this Picture: Kodak's 30-year Slide into Bankruptcy." *Knowledge@Wharton.* February 1, 2012. Accessed on June 12, 2021, https://knowledge.wharton.upenn.edu/article/whats-wrong-with-this-picture-kodaks-30-year-slide-into-bankruptcy/.

CHAPTER 10

Bezos, Jeff. *Invent & Wander.* Boston: Harvard Business Review Press, 2021.

Burtsell, Richard. *The Catholic Encyclopedia.* Volume 1. New York: Robert Appleton Company, 1907. Accessed June 12, 2021, http://www.newadvent.org/cathen/01168b.htm.

Carter, Alexandra. *Ask for More.* New York: Simon & Schuster, 2020.

Deighton, John. "How Snapple Got Its Juice Back." *Harvard Business Review,* January 2002. Accessed June 12, 2021, https://hbr.org/2002/01/how-snapple-got-its-juice-back.

Dell, Michael. *Direct from Dell.* New York: Harper Collins, 1999.

Emmi, Joseph. "At Amazon despite all the data, anecdotes still winning arguments." *The Bridge blog.* May 7, 2018. Accessed June 12, 2021, https://medium.com/the-bridge/at-amazon-despite-all-the-data-anecdotes-still-winning-arguments-875ddaac3f3f.

Garvin, David A and Michael A. Roberto. "What You Don't Know About Making Decisions." *Harvard Business Review,* August 2001. Accessed June 12, 2021, https://hbr.org/2001/09/what-you-dont-know-about-making-decisions.

Goodwin, Doris Kearns. *Team of Rivals: The Political Genius of Abraham Lincoln.* New York: Simon & Schuster, 2006.

Grove, Andy. *Only the Paranoid Survive/* New York: Currency, 1999.

Hayward, Mathew L.A, and Donald C. Hambrick. "Explaining the Premiums Paid for Large Acquisitions: Evidence of CEO Hubris." *Administrative Science Quarterly.* March 1997. Volume 42, No. 1. Accessed June 12, 2021, https://psycnet.apa.org/record/1997-04512-002.

Heath, Chip and Dan Heath. *Decisive.* New York: Currency, 2013.

Hoffman, Bryce G. *American Icon: Alan Mulally and the Fight to Save Ford Motor Company.* New York: Crown Business, 2012.

Korgerus, Mikael and Roman Tschappeler. *The Decision Book.* New York: W.W. Norton & Company, 2017.

Krishnamurthy, Balaji. "Consensus is the Road to Mediocrity." *ThinkShift White Paper.* Accessed June 12, 2021.

Jin, Brenda. "Guanyin Labs founder Brenda Jin on how data drives results" *PluralSight blog.* Accessed June 12, 2021, https://www.pluralsight.com/blog/teams/driving-better-outcomes-through-data-with-brenda-jin.

Nutt, Paul C. "Expanding the Search for Alternatives during Strategic Decision Making." *Academy of Management Executive,* November 2004. Accessed June 12, 2021, https://www.jstor.org/stable/4166121?seq=1.

Rivlin, Gary. "He Naps. He Sings. And He Isn't Michael Dell." *The New York Times,* September 11, 2005. Accessed June 12, 2021, https://www.nytimes.com/2005/09/11/technology/he-naps-he-sings-and-he-isnt-michael-dell.html.

Scott, Kim. *Radical Candor.* New York: St. Martin's Press, 2019.

Thaler, Richard. *Misbehaving.* New York: W. W. Norton & Company, 2015.

The Arbinger Institute. *The Out-ward Mindset: How to change lives and transform organizations.* San Francisco: Berrett-Koehler Publishers, 2016.

Tinsley, Catherine H, Robin L. Dillon, and Peter M. Madsen. "How to Avoid Catastrophe." *Harvard Business Review,* April 2011. Accessed June 12, 2021, https://hbr.org/2011/04/how-to-avoid-catastrophe.

Torres, Monica. "Simon Sinek explains why you should be the last to speak in a meeting." *The Ladders.* January 8, 2018. Accessed June 12, 2021, https://www.theladders.com/career-advice/simon-sinek-explains-why-bosses-need-to-be-the-last-to-speak-in-a-meeting.

CHAPTER 11

Carnahan, Dustin, Qi Hao, Xiaoya Jian, and Heysung Lee. "Feeling Fine about Being Wrong: The Influence of Self-Affirmation on the Effectiveness of Corrective Information." *Human Communication Research*, Volume 44, Issue 3, July 2018. Accessed June 12, 2021, https://doi.org/10.1093/hcr/hqy001.

Davis, Jennifer. "Beyond Wishful Thinking: Visa's Chris Curtin on Sales and Marketing Alignment." *Forbes,* July 16, 2018. Accessed June 12, 2021, https://www.forbes.com/sites/jenniferdavis/2018/07/16/beyond-wishful-thinking-visas-chris-curtin-on-sales-and-marketing-alignment/?sh=3ca30aa468ee.

Gensler, Art. *Art's Principles: 50 years of hard-learned lessons in building a world-class professional services firm.* New York: Wilson Lafferty, 2015.

"Google Buys YouTube for $1.65 billion." *The Associated Press.* October 9, 2006. Accessed June 12, 2021, https://www.nbcnews.com/id/wbna15196982.

Grant, Adam. *Think Again.* New York: Viking, 2021.

Grove, Andy. *Only the Paranoid Survive.* New York: Currency, 1996.

Howard, Caroline. "Google's Susan Wojcicki Takes Lead Of Ads And Engineerin.g" *Forbes,* May 6, 2011. Accessed on June 12, 2021, https://www.forbes.com/sites/carolinehoward/2011/05/06/googles-susan-wojcicki-suddenly-lead-of-engineering-and-ads-she-wants-to-talk-about-chickens/?sh=ae146e479eae.

Kübler-Ross, Elizabeth and David Kessler. *On Grief and Grieving.* New York: Scribner, 2014.

Madigan, Tim. *I'm Proud of You: My Friendship with Fred Rodgers.* Los Angeles: Ubuntu Books, 2012.

Schapp, Pieter. "The 4 levels of data maturity that you should absolutely know about." *Computd.* March 16, 2020. Accessed on June 12, 2021, https://computd.nl/demystification/4-levels-of-data-maturity/.

TED. "Tim Ferris: Why you should define your fears instead of your goals." April 2017. Accessed June 12, 2021, https://www.ted.com/talks/tim_ferriss_why_you_should_define_your_fears_instead_of_your_goals.

Thaler, Richard. *Misbehaving.* New York: W. W. Norton, 2015.

WHYY. "Why do we hate to fail?" *PBS.* July 30, 2015. Accessed June 12, 2021, https://whyy.org/segments/why-do-we-hate-to-fail/.

CHAPTER 12

Calore, Michael. "Twitter is Ruling SXSW." *Wired,* March 2007. Accessed on June 12, 2021, https://www.wired.com/2007/03/twitter-is-ruling-sxsw/.

Collins, Jim. "Best New Year's Resolution? A 'Stop Doing' List." *USA Today,* December 30, 2003. Accessed June 12, 2021, https://

www.jimcollins.com/article_topics/articles/best-new-years.html.

Garber, Megan. "Instagram was first called 'Burbn'." *The Atlantic,* July 2, 2014. Accessed on June 12, 2021, https://www.theatlantic.com/technology/archive/2014/07/instagram-used-to-be-called-brbn/373815/.

Harper, Justin. "Jack Dorsey's first ever tweet sells for $2.9m." BBC News, March 23, 2021. Accessed June 12, 2021, https://www.bbc.com/news/business-56492358.

Hutchings, Lucy. "Margaret Thatcher's Most Famous Quotes." *Vogue,* April 8, 2013. Accessed June 12, 2021, https://www.vogue.co.uk/gallery/margaret-thatcher-most-famous-quotes.

Hyter, Michael C. *The Power of Choice: Embracing Efficacy to Drive Your Career.* New York: Global Novations, 2011.

Koehn, Nancy. *Brand New.* Boston: Harvard Business School Press, 2001.

Lauder, Leonard A. *The Company I Keep: My Life in Beauty.* New York: HarperCollins, 2020.

Meisenzahl, Mary. "Instagram's founder on whether he'd sell to Facebook again: 'When someone comes and offers you a billion dollars for 11 people, what do you say?'." *Business Insider,* November 6, 2019. Acessed on June 12, 2021, https://www.businessinsider.com/instagram-kevin-systrom-would-sell-to-facebook-again-2019-11.

Newkirk II, Vann R. "The American Idea in 140 Characters." *The Atlantic,* March 25, 2016. Accessed June 12, 2021, https://www.theatlantic.com/politics/archive/2016/03/twitter-politics-last-decade/475131/.

Reed, Rob. "The Kat Cole Story: Unlikely Success At The Intersection Of Hooters And Cinnabon." *Forbes,* August 26, 2020. Accessed June 12, 2021, https://www.forbes.com/sites/robreed/2020/08/26/the-kat-cole-story-unlikely-success-at-the-intersection-of-hooters-and-cinnabon/#4f4b6b781a84.

Sawyer, Keith. *Zig Zag: The Surprising Path to Greater Creativity.* New York: Jossey-Bass, 2013.

Swift, James. "SXSW14: Twitter Crashes during Biz Stone talk." *Campaign Live.* March 12, 2014. Accessed on June 12, 2021, https://www.campaignlive.com/article/sxsw14-twitter-crashes-during-biz-stone-talk/1284704.

TFL. "What is the 'lipstick index' and why it it important right now?" *The Fashion Law,* August 1, 2017. Accessed June 12, 2021, https://www.thefashionlaw.com/premium-beauty-what-is-it-and-why-is-it-so-important-right-now/.

Wagner, Kurt. "Here's why Facebook's $1 billion Instagram acquisition was such a great deal." *recode.* April 9, 2017. Accessed on June 12, 2021, https://www.vox.com/2017/4/9/15235940/facebook-instagram-acquisition-anniversary.

CHAPTER 13

"About." Mike McHargue Website. Accessed June 12, 2021, https://mikemchargue.com/about.

Aurelius, Marcus and Gregory Hays, *Meditations: a New Translation.* New York: Random House Publishing Group, 2003.

Berger, Jonah. *Contagious.* New York: Simon & Schuster, 2013.

Caplow, Beth. "Three Seismic Shifts in Buying Behavior from Forrester's 2021 B2B Buying Study." *Forrester website.* April 14, 2021. Accessed June 12, 2021, https://go.forrester.com/blogs/three-seismic-shifts-in-buying-behavior-from-forresters-2021-b2b-buying-survey/.

Emond, Larry. "Maintaining a Culture of Builders and Innovators at Amazon: a conversation with Beth Galetti." *Gallup Workplace CHRO Conversations.* February 26, 2018. Accessed June 12, 2021, https://www.gallup.com/workplace/231635/maintaining-culture-builders-innovators-amazon.aspx.

Hemerling, Jim, Julie Kilmann, Martin Daneosastro, Liza Stutts, and Cailin Ahern. "It's Not a Digital Transformation Without a

Digital Culture." *Boston Consulting Group (BCG)*. April 13, 2018. Accessed June 12, 2021, https://www.bcg.com/en-us/publications/2018/not-digital-transformation-without-digital-culture.

Hiatt, Jeffrey M. *ADKAR: A Model for Change in Business, Government, and our Community*. Boulder, Colorado: Jeffrey M. Hiatt, 2006.

Miller, Donald. *Building a Story Brand*. New York: Harper Collins Leadership, 2017.

"NetFlix historic stock price." Macrotrends. Accessed June 12, 2021, https://www.macrotrends.net/stocks/charts/NFLX/netflix/stock-price-history.

Peters, Kurt. "Walmart.com enters the DVD movie rental business." *DigitalCommerce360*, October 15, 2002. Accessed June 12, 2021, https://www.digitalcommerce360.com/2002/10/15/walmart-com-enters-the-dvd-movie-rental-business/.

Regan, Keith. "Netflix Taking Over Wal-Mart's Online DVD Rental Business." *eCommerce Times*, May 19, 2005. Accessed June 12, 2021, https://www.ecommercetimes.com/story/43221.html.

Smith, Thomas. *Successful Advertising*. London: Thomas Smith Agency, 1885.

Struck, Brooke. "How Fun Might Move the World: Cass Sunstein." *The Decision Corner Podcast*. September 2, 2020. Accessed June 12, 2021, https://thedecisionlab.com/podcasts/how-fun-might-move-the-world/.

Tamer, Delly. "The art of making great decisions—Netflix's daredevil bet when it was a tiny start-up." *LinkedIn Pulse*. November 30, 2020. Accessed June 12, 2021, https://www.linkedin.com/pulse/art-making-great-decisions-netflixs-daredevil-bet-when-delly-tamer/.

TED. "Uri Hasson: This is Your Brain on Communication." February 2016. Accessed June 12, 2021, https://www.ted.com/talks/uri_hasson_this_is_your_brain_on_communication#t-20902.

CHAPTER 14

"M&A Statistics." *Institute of Mergers, Acquisitions, and Alliances (IMAA)*. Accessed June 12, 2021, https://imaa-institute.org/mergers-and-acquisitions-statistics/

"M&A Trends Survey: the future of M&A." Deloitte. 2018. Accessed June 12, 2021, https://www2.deloitte.com/us/en/pages/mergers-and-acquisitions/articles/m-a-trends-report.html#infographic.

Gavin, Matt. "What are Mergers & Acquisitions? 4 Key Risks." *Harvard Business School Online Blog.* July 25, 2019. Accessed June 12, 2021, https://online.hbs.edu/blog/post/mergers-and-acquisitions.

Maxwell, John C. *Talent Is Never Enough: Discover the Choices That Will Take You Beyond Your Talent.* New York: Thomas Nelson, 2007.